The Humanities in the Schools

A Contemporary Symposium

Edited by Harold Taylor

Former President, Sarah Lawrence College

Citation Press, New York · 1968

For reprint permission, grateful acknowledgment is made to:

College Entrance Examination Board, New York, for "The School as a Social Environment" by Edgar Z. Friedenberg from COLLEGE ADMISSIONS 10; THE BEHAVIORAL SCIENCES AND EDUCATION, published in 1963 by the College Entrance Examination Board, New York.

Harper & Row, Publishers for "Lit. Instructor" from TRAVELING THROUGH THE DARK by William Stafford. Copyright © 1958 by William Stafford.

Random House, Inc. for "Subject: Object: Sentence" from SELECTED POEMS OF STEPHEN SPENDER. © copyright 1964 by Stephen Spender.

Photographs by Ivan J. Klebanow

Design by June Martin

Library of Congress Catalog Card Number 68-29402

1st printing September 1968

Printed in the U.S.A.

Contents

Preface   9

Participants in the Symposium   13

The Arts and the Humanities, *Harold Taylor*   17

Where to Begin, *Harold Rosenberg*   69

Language as Communication, *Stephen Spender*   83

Films and the Future, *Stanley Kauffmann*   99

The Conservative Arts, *Robert Shaw*   115

A Teaching Credential for
    Philoctetes?, *Edgar Z. Friedenberg*   139

Some Ideas for Action, *Harold Taylor*   164

Contributors   171

Preface

OVER A PERIOD OF TWO DAYS in December of 1965 at
the University of Kentucky, six of us—Edgar Friedenberg, Stanley Kauffmann, Harold Rosenberg, Robert
Shaw, Stephen Spender, and I—presented papers in a
symposium on the arts and the humanities which I had
invited the others to attend. The symposium had been
organized at the invitation of Professor Richard Miller
of the College of Education of the University of Kentucky. Its purpose was to bring together a congenial
group of people whose main business is with the arts
and letters, to see what ideas could be developed
among us for making the arts and humanistic studies
flourish more vigorously in the public schools and in
the colleges and universities. We felt that if people who
were not themselves professional educators could turn
their minds to the question of what they would like to
see happen about the arts and humanities in the schools,

something fresh and educationally useful might come of it.

Each paper at the symposium was followed by discussion in which we were joined by fifteen other participants, most of whom knew more about the practical problems of teaching in the schools than we did. Although the six writers had had experience of varying lengths of time in teaching college students and others, only Edgar Friedenberg among us had had direct and continuing experience in the schools, through his research and writing about high school students.

This meant that we were all free to say whatever we thought should be done with the arts and humanities in the schools without any direct knowledge of why it could or couldn't be done, and without having been trained to do it in any particular way. At the same time, we had the advantage of hearing our ideas discussed by colleagues who knew what obstacles and possibilities existed in the schools that might hinder or help the ideas to find their way into action.

I wish that more conferences about educational problems could have this kind of advantage. I have found that at most conferences of educators, the people who attend are all so familiar with the way things are done and so absorbed in the practical questions of the present curriculum and organization that after a while all the conferences seem to be the same one—they all have the same agenda, use the same language, and employ an interchangeable set of people to make the speeches and speak on the panels.

At one stage of the Kentucky discussions we were talking about why art is so often corrupted by being made into an academic subject in the colleges and schools and of the danger in leaving the arts in the hands of educators who don't understand them. Harold Rosenberg pointed out that it is only very recently that artists and writers had ever been invited to conferences on education. "We had conferences," said Rosenberg, "although we didn't call them that, and we didn't have them with *you*. We just talked about the things artists like to talk about."

Edgar Friedenberg remarked at another point that the purpose of educational conferences was for the participants to make a record of their own status and to be seen with other people. In any institutional arrangement for education, conferences included, he said, it is almost impossible to tell the truth, since so much is at stake in the existing institutional programs that to talk about them freely, honestly, and critically would be to threaten those who made them and to break the conventions of polite discourse in the educational community.

That did not turn out to be a problem at the Kentucky conference. As the symposium went along, it became clear to all of us that whatever might be the merit of Friedenberg's sociology of conferences, the plan for bringing artists and writers together to talk with school teachers and educators about what should be done with the arts and the humanities in the schools worked very well. Some of the discussion was brilliant, all of it uninhibited, and fresh ideas from outside the educational system were brought into a situation in which those who were inside it could feel perfectly free to talk about the merits of the ideas of the outsiders, and the outsiders could say what they thought without annoying the insiders. No matter what disagreements we found among ourselves as we discussed the papers, the force of argument, the pressure of concern, and the seriousness with which the participants addressed themselves to the questions they had been asked to consider, moved all of us toward a clearer understanding of what the issues were.

It seemed to those who took part that it might be useful to others who share our interest in the arts and education to have a chance to read the papers and to have an account of what went on in the discussions. We are therefore publishing the original papers in this book, with an introductory chapter that includes most of my own paper, "The Arts and the Humanities," with which the symposium began, and a review of the main issues and some of the things which were said during the two days of discussion. Our thanks go to the University of Kentucky under whose auspices the symposium was held, to Professor Richard Miller, who first suggested the symposium and made the practical arrangements for it, to Westab, Inc., who financed it, and to the participants who kept us informed and instructed about the educational realities.

HAROLD TAYLOR
New York City
April 1968

Participants in the Symposium

Contributors of Papers:

  Edgar Friedenberg, Sociologist

  Stanley Kauffmann, Literary and Film Critic

  Harold Rosenberg, Art Critic

  Robert Shaw, Conductor

  Stephen Spender, Poet and Writer

  Harold Taylor, Author, Educator, and Symposium
    Chairman

Participants in the Discussion:

  Howard Conant, Chairman
  Department of Art Education
  New York University

Harriet Eisner, Artist

Murray Eisner, Vice-President, Marketing
Montag, Inc., Division of Westab, Inc.

George P. Elliott, Writer

Bernard Fitzgerald, Professor of Music
University of Kentucky

Richard A. Gibboney, Commissioner of Education
State Department of Education, Montpelier, Vermont

Mrs. Maxine Greene, Editor, *Teachers College Record,*
and Professor of English
Teachers College, Columbia University

Harlan Hoffa, Specialist in Art Education
Arts and Humanities Branch, U.S. Office of
Education

Charles R. Keller, Director
John Hay Fellows Program

Miss Nancy Larrick, Writer and Educator

Lewis Leary, Chairman
Department of English and Comparative Literature
Columbia University

Paul C. Nagel, Dean
College of Arts and Sciences, University of Kentucky

Dan C. Pinck, Deputy Director and Secretary of the
    Corporation
Educational Services, Inc.

Thomas F. Powell, Assistant Professor of Social
    Science and Education
Maxwell Graduate School of Citizenship and Public
    Affairs
Syracuse University

Ira Singleton, Music Editor
Silver Burdett Company

HAROLD TAYLOR

The Arts and the Humanities

ONE OF THE DIFFICULTIES with American culture is that too few people know what it is and assume that a cultured person, or a person with culture, is one who is well-mannered, reads good books, goes to the opera, and speaks without raising his voice. The Untutored, the Uneducated, the Uncultured, people with no background, all belong to another category. Culture is a word associated with social class and the social graces, which misconstrues the true meaning of what it is.

Ortega put the matter bluntly:

> Our ideas — that is culture. The present crisis is less a crisis of culture than of the position we have given to culture. We have set it before and above life, when it ought to be behind and below life — because it is a reaction to life. We must now stop putting the cart before the horse.

We have not stopped putting the cart before the horse. We have simply put more into the cart and are now saying that the horse, no matter what his position, front or back, should pull harder and faster. The cart in this case is the curriculum of the high school and college. It is already jammed with excess baggage to which it is now proposed to add more, a different kind of baggage called the humanities. The horse is the student, driven by an educational system which has mistakenly put the curriculum in front and the student behind while expecting him to pull it along after him.

So much for the metaphor. Put in plain terms, the American system of education has given a position to the arts which divorces them from the living experience of the young and turns them into objects and activities to be described in humanities courses, surveys of art history, and similar diversions. As Ortega puts it, this sets culture before and above life, when it ought to be behind and below life — because it is a reaction to life, whatever the life may be, in the society, or the suburbs, or among the rural and urban poor. The roots of culture are in the events and experiences of one's own life, and the culture itself is a name for the body of ideas, experiences, and customs to which the members of a given community adapt themselves — the things they accept as valid and according to which they live their lives.

The real problem is to recapture the originality of one's own direct experience, so that the emotional habits and intellectual customs which grow up over the years and are accepted as proper and necessary ways of behaving can be refreshed by new ways of responding to whatever has become customary. This is especially true of the response to art. Once it has been established by educational authorities that certain kinds of art are to be looked at, heard, seen, or otherwise experienced in certain ways, once categories have been laid down and generalizations made about what kind of art falls into this or that kind of classification, the student no longer has the responsibility or even the desire to observe the art object in a personal way. He has been told what to think about it, what to feel about it, and how to classify it. If he learns his lesson well, he can assure himself that he has a grip on culture, that he has passed his examination in sensibility, and can then rest content with his inclusion among those who have been liberally educated.

For it is easier, both for educators and for the persons to whom education is done, to classify the objects and occasions of aesthetic experience in a systematic way than to learn how to experience the occasion and the object for oneself. As Theodore Flournay once said in a comment about William James:[1]

The artistic mind looks at everything in its concrete particularity and presents it as individual, while the scientific intellect analyzes, abstracts, and generalizes. All science is general, as Aristotle said, and when it deals with particular objects it at once dissolves their particularity. . . . But it is just this unique individuality, intact, immediate, and real, which is the exclusive interest of art. . . .

1. Theodore Flournay, *The Philosophy of William James,* translated by Edwin B. Holt and William James, Jr., 1917, pp. 4, as quoted in Gay Wilson Allen, *William James* (New York: Viking Press, 1967).

This is the real point. Systems of education, like systems of science, tend to dissolve the particularity of the individual, to assume, for example, that all students are alike, and in the very effort to form a system through which each can be educated, to defeat the individual's capacity to learn for himself. This can be seen in the standard practice of educators who assemble students into classrooms and courses and present them with organized bodies of subject matter, rather than turning them loose in a variety of groups and a variety of situations where they can carry out their own explorations and personal experiences in art and ideas.

Learning is equally personal when it is done right. It is only when teaching and learning are thought of as *education* that it all becomes impersonal and over-organized. To keep education and the culture alive and growing, it is necessary that all the ideas they contain be rethought, reshaped, reexperienced, and placed in a new perspective from year to year and generation to generation by each new entrant into the world. It should be the aim of education to create the conditions out of which there can come a constant renewal of insight and re-creation of ideas and values in the personal lives of the young and their teachers.

The nature of justice, for example, has its perennial necessities and modes; these can be found in the classical texts. But the nature of justice for the Negro in America, to choose an instance, or the Chinese in Indonesia, has its actual meaning in the lives and experiences of contemporary Negroes and Whites, Chinese and Indonesians, within the context of their society. Justice is an activity, a situation, a series of feelings, ideas, and acts which take place in a personal and social context, and it is not possible to understand its nature without knowing the reality of existing individuals who act justly or who experience justice or injustice. Beauty and aesthetic quality are no different. The nature and form of the arts can be read about and pointed out in the classical texts and models, but the true nature of art and its attributes can only be found through immediate experiences, feelings, ideas, and acts.

For that reason I question the whole idea of the "humanities" as a special area of the curriculum designed to take care of human values which, presumably, the rest of the curriculum can then safely ignore while it goes on ladling out its generous supply of facts. The humanities are not culture-containers, or value-containers, or courses in the higher things. In one sense there is no such thing as the humanities, unless we are willing to accept the idea that science is not a humanistic discipline and that facts have nothing to do with values. Science is an activity of thought whose main characteristic is an insistence on understanding, more precisely than is possible by any other means, the nature of a reality that would otherwise be perceived in personal terms and without the particular kind of precision which science brings to its tasks. Science is a branch of philosophy, the branch that makes theories and investigates phenomena. It therefore has a great deal to do with philosophy, and it is no accident that most of the great philosophers of the nineteenth and twentieth centuries have been scientists and that their predecessors thought of science as a branch of natural philosophy.

On the other hand, we do have to do something with the kind of raw material of human experience that does not lend itself to being organized into the concepts and categories of the scientific disciplines. We have to deal with matters of the heart, of the senses, of the deepening of consciousness itself. There is a need here for looser and different categories and a different kind of precision. There is a need for ways of putting together the results of personal insight and of spontaneous perception into forms that can make them available to others. The artists and the writers find ways of doing this through whatever forms they develop — in novels, paintings, plays, stories, poems, dances, and the rest — and the scholars and educators then have the obligation to find ways in which the work of the artists and writers can be opened up to those who may not have thought about or felt what the artists have been feeling and thinking or have not been interested at all in what the artists have been doing.

In this sense the scholars and educators are organizers of experience, their own and that of others whom they teach. At their best, they are sensitive enough and informed enough to put their students into situations in which the ideas and images of painters, playwrights, philosophers, historians, or dancers have a chance to enter fully the consciousness of the students. This means the engagement of students in the practice of the arts themselves and the confrontation of students with genuine issues involving genuine intellectual, moral, and aesthetic options. The student must face the fact that it is he who must decide the character and quality of his own response to an object of art; it is he who must judge the worth of an idea within a framework of his own values, a framework he must learn to construct for himself.

The trouble is that in the schools and colleges he is very seldom allowed to do so. Except in a sprinkling of experimental institutions, the concept of personal involvement and confrontation with issues and ideas is not a central mode of educational philosophy. All the answers are given before the student has a chance to ask about anything. The organization of knowledge becomes more a matter of administrative convenience than of educational imagination, and little attention is given to the natural ways in which students can learn to enter into the experience of the arts and society and can form their own conclusions about what they find there.

We may, of course, use the words, art, science, history, philosophy, sociology, and literature to describe certain bodies of knowledge which are grouped together by convention, and we can separate the arts and the humanities from the natural and social sciences simply by naming them as separate items and assembling materials under the proper subject-matter headings. But it is crucial to remember that in doing this scholars and educators are organizing knowledge in order to distribute it and that the names of the subjects do not correspond to the areas of experience out of which they were first created.

Was Socrates studying and teaching political science, psychology, Greek philosophy, or linguistics? His general reputation has come down as a philosopher, but he talked about everything, including education. He did not talk or think in separate categories. He talked about whatever interested him, and he was interested in inquiry of all kinds. He pursued answers wherever his mind took him. So do novelists, painters, playwrights, and so should students.

I mention Socrates at this point because I can recall a controversy at the University of Wisconsin when I taught in the philosophy department there, about whether the political science department should be allowed to teach Plato and Hobbes, since Plato and Hobbes belonged to the philosophy courses and it was held by some that the political science people should stick to their own authors. I suggested that we trade Hobbes for Marx and that we would probably come out ahead.

Then the absurd question for the college curriculum becomes: Would Plato's *Republic*, taught in the political science department, be part of the student's education in the humanities or would that simply be plain social science, with the student thereby robbed of the delicate philosophical insight available only in the philosophy department — an agency of learning properly certified as a legitimate source of values rather than of grubby facts?

We are face to face here with one of the major obstacles to educational reform, and with the source of much educational subversion. The student is made to stand at the counter of the academic bureaucracy, counting up his credits in the humanities in order to be certified as having been made properly aware of the great questions of life and history. Yet the primary purpose of true education in every field is humanistic and consists in the achievement of insight, the ability to distinguish truth from falsehood, and the ability to deal seriously with the intricacies and ambiguities of good and evil, beauty and ugliness, belief and disbelief. The study of psychology, for instance, should be a means of discovering the nature of man, not an exercise in going through a textbook.

It is true of course that the gigantic body of knowledge accumulated through two thousand years of collecting must be divided, subdivided, classified, and organized if it is to be at all manageable. But making it manageable is not merely the obligation of scholars and teachers, it is also the obligation of students, and the reason for presenting the subject matter to them is to provide the means through which they can learn to enter the stream of cultural and social history without having to collect the entire body of knowledge all over again with every generation. The body of knowledge is a medium for creative and analytic thinking. It exists as material through which learning can take place, not merely as material to be learned.

My proposal is, therefore, that we return to the root of the matter, in the quality and variety of experience available to the race, and that we consider education in the humanities not as a problem of developing a separate set of courses in a separate section of the curriculum, but as the creation of a spirit of inquiry and aesthetic interest throughout the whole curriculum and the entire environment of the school or college. The arts themselves must be a central element in that environment. In the time of the Renaissance it was the creation of new modes of perception and sensibility, a new way of looking at the world by poets, writers, painters, sculptors, architects, and thinkers that broke the chains of orthodox philosophy and the conventional wisdom. The spirit of humanism, of enlightenment, then as now, is to be found in the sensibility of the artist, the scholar, the student, and the citizen, all of them using their resources as creators, critics, audience, and learners, each with his own function, each learning from the other, each willing to accept what is human as the locus of ultimate concern.

Herbert Read has a direct way of putting it when he speaks of the necessity to preserve the natural intensity of all modes of perception and sensation. The sheer delight in perceiving objects and ideas which have in them the capacity to evoke response, the intellectual excitement of apprehending ideas which make a difference to the way one looks at oneself and at the world, the elation of intense involvement in work of one's own in science, in art, in teaching, or in organizing a body of knowledge which has personal meaning because it has become one's own through effort — these are the values the schools must seek and around which the curriculum must be formed. The curriculum is the whole atmosphere generated by the students and teachers together. Its qualities are determined by what the students are encouraged to do and how the teacher teaches, how he chooses the variety of experiences he makes available to his students. These decisions on his part are determined by the quality of his own sensibility and the degree of his concern.

I am thinking here not necessarily about teachers

who are said to be "inspiring," although God knows we need them, but of teachers who are themselves sensitive to the values and inner meanings of the arts and sciences, who have entered fully into the task of creating a body of knowledge of their own in which they take pleasure and satisfaction. There is no reason why every student and every teacher should possess the same body of knowledge. What each man knows is what he has paid a price for learning, what he has found for himself, and this can, should, and does vary from person to person, depending on the influences and opportunities that surround him and on the initiative he has learned to take.

Accordingly, when we speak of the new organizations which have grown up these past few years in the United States, ranging from the State Arts Councils and the National Endowments for the Arts and for the Humanities to the arts centers and fine arts departments on the college and university campuses, we are recognizing in general terms that new forms of organization are now necessary if the arts are to flourish in the communities and in the lives of Americans. For many reasons the interest of the public in the arts has increased a great deal faster than it has in the schools and colleges, until now the demands for culture and art to put into the culture centers and for education to get people to go there have outstripped the capacity of the educational system to provide either the artists or the educated audiences.

That is why it is crucially important that educators who are now being called upon to do something about the arts and the humanities in the schools should know what it is they are dealing with. When the movement for government support of the arts and the humanities first began to develop, the only real political constituency for pushing the legislation lay in the universities and the professional academic organizations, along with a limited number of artists and writers who believed in the idea that the government should take responsibility for helping the arts and artists. School teachers were not involved, nor were the schools themselves.

As the legislation was being written by interested persons inside and outside the Congress, one central issue emerged — the distinction between the arts and the humanities, with the artists and writers taking the view that the creative arts had their own place in the culture and must not be lumped together with the "humanities," an over-all term for what the academic profession considers to be the province of humanistic scholarship. In the beginning the tendency was to form a government foundation, similar in style to the National Science Foundation, with the arts included in the over-all structure. What seemed to me then, and what has turned out to be, the wisdom of the artists, prevailed, and two endowments were organized — one for the arts, the other for the humanities.

The language of the legislation which determined the two areas indicates what you are likely to get when you make the separation. The humanities, as defined in the Arts and Humanities Act of 1965, include, but are not limited to, the study of "language, both modern and classic, linguistics, literature, history, jurisprudence, philosophy, archaeology, the history, criticism, theory, and practice of the arts, and those aspects of the social sciences which have humanistic content and employ humanisitic methods." On the other hand, the arts, as defined, include, but are not limited to, "music (instrumental and vocal), dance, drama, folk art, creative writing, architecture and allied fields, painting, sculpture, photography, graphic and craft arts, industrial design, costume and fashion design, motion pictures, television, radio, tape and sound recording, and the arts related to the presentation, performance, execution, and exhibition of such major art forms." The problem then is, how do we get all these, or any major part of them, into the schools?

For the purposes of the schools, according to the United States Office of Education, the humanities and the arts "comprise all those subjects in the elementary and secondary school programs which involve the student in the consideration of aesthetic, social, and ethical values." In practice this means that once more the distinction between the arts and the humanities has been blurred, and, with the inclusion of social with aesthetic and ethical values, almost anything in the curriculum other than the natural sciences, which also possess social values, is included in the arts and the humanities. In practice it also means that the professional academic definition of the humanities has prevailed and that they are considered to be academic, scholarly, and professional studies rather than activities in the field of the arts and letters which can rouse up the aesthetic, ethical, and moral enthusiasms of young people in the process of being liberally educated.

It is therefore encouraging to note that one of the first matching grants made by the Humanities Endowment was to establish a Commission on the Humanities in the Schools, that direct liaison has been made with the Humanities and Arts Division of the U.S. Office of Education and other government agencies, that some experimental programs in the arts for slum children have been set in motion, and that attention has been given to improving the quality of teaching in the colleges through fellowships for teaching interneships. But these are very small first steps; the bulk of the Endowment grants are for academic research in the conventional fields.

The U.S. Office of Education has gone farther and has faced the fact that the present school curriculum is in a state of imbalance, with a heavy emphasis on academic courses suitable for meeting college admission requirements, especially in the sciences, taught in such a way that the material is stripped of its humanistic content. I quote from a document published by the Office of Education entitled *Instructional Objectives in the Humanities,* which lays out some goals with which the schools are asked to come to terms:

- To introduce all students (including the vocationally minded who will not go beyond high school) to the study of man — his nature, the full development of his faculties, the realization of his aspirations, and the securing of his well-being.

- To help the student come to know himself, to understand what has shaped his beliefs, attitudes, and fortunes, and to develop a critical sense which will allow him as an individual to select and preserve the best in human societies.

• To develop in the student an attitude toward life which centers on the inherent dignity of each individual human being.

• To help the student reconcile individual freedom with social control.

• To cultivate his understanding of the unresolved conflicts and struggles that have persisted throughout human history.

• To develop his understanding of how social relations between different segments of society condition the form and content of literature and the arts.

• To develop in the student an understanding of how language shapes ideas within a culture and is at the same time an expression of that culture.

• To give the student the experience of personal involvement with ideas that have moved and shaped human societies.

In announcing these objectives, the U.S. Office of Education, whether it means to or not, is calling for a radical reform in the entire elementary and high school curriculum to restore to it "the consideration of aesthetic, social, and ethical values," a consideration which is in fact the central purpose of liberal education itself and one which should run through the whole curriculum and intellectual life of the school. In the long run, no matter how much cultural activity is carried on outside the educational institutions, the only place where fundamental understanding and support of the arts and the humanities can be created is inside the educational system. This means that educating teachers in an awareness of the meaning of humanistic studies, "the experience of personal involvement with ideas that have moved and shaped human societies," and "the study of man — his nature, the full development of his faculties, the realization of his aspirations, and the securing of his well-being," are the prime considerations for any plans to be made in educational reform, in the humanities, or in anything else.

It is therefore all the more regrettable that the emphasis of the Humanities Endowment and of most organizations connected with the humanities should be on more of the same for scholars in the academic disciplines, with the usual concentration of such scholars in the graduate schools, and their subsequent divorce from the intellectual and aesthetic needs of undergraduates and high school students. Since it is in the undergraduate courses in the arts and humanities that teachers are prepared for service in the schools, this means that there is little connection between the support given to the humanities in general and the drastic need for humanistic education in the elementary and secondary schools.

When the problem of mass culture in a democracy is examined closely, it becomes clear that one of the major difficulties in the way of overcoming its banality lies in the anti-aesthetic and in many ways anti-intellectual content of the curricula of the high schools and universities. The creative arts are pushed out of the high school curriculum in favor of those subjects necessary for gaining admission to college; they are pushed out of college in favor of those subjects necessary for graduate school. Everything becomes a prerequirement for everything else, and the arts, not being a requirement for anything except themselves and a certain kind of joy, are excluded from the regular curriculum. Now my fear is that they too will be made into academic requirements of the same kind as the others and that the arts will be destroyed by being taught about in humanities courses, since humanities courses in the high school borrow their style—the Great Books, survey courses in philosophy or "Western Civilization," surveys of art history — from the courses already taught in the colleges.

Where is there room for the students whose gifts are not purely scholastic? Where is there room for the child who loves to paint, to sculpt, to sing, to dance, to act, to compose, to write, to celebrate his personal joy? Or, for that matter, where is there in the educational system a concern for the majority of American children who have never been close enough to the live arts to know what they are?

In the nursery school and kindergarten the arts flourish naturally, since they provide so natural and unavoidable a way for the child to learn; there is no need to cut up the curriculum into subject matter. But very early in the elementary grades the external values of the society begin to impose themselves on the curriculum and on the children, and the child is asked to adapt himself to the norms determined by the demands of his society. Few of these demands, until now, have had to do with the demonstration of an aesthetic sensitivity.

The point is made by William Stafford in the beginning lines of his poem, "Lit Instructor."[2]

Day after day up there beating my wings
with all of the softness truth requires
I feel them shrug whenever I pause:
they class my voice among tentative things,

And they credit fact, force, battering.
I dance my way toward the family of knowing,
embracing stray error as a long-lost boy
and bringing him home with my fluttering. . . .

The truth of the artist does require softness, sympathy, concern, and a certain kind of attention which, if not given or induced, means that his truth remains unavailable to his audience. That this attention is seldom given in the high school and college can be explained by the fact that it is so seldom asked for. It is not hard to imagine the examination questions which would afflict a student who had "studied" Stafford's poem: "Why is error like a long-lost boy?" "Can you feel a shrug?"

The course of instruction in the literary arts is a continual stream of interruptions in the student's learning, interruptions to inquire of him what he has remem-

2. William Stafford, *Traveling Through the Dark* (New York: Harper & Row, 1962), p. 38.

bered and what are the facts. The student, therefore, becomes accustomed to listening and thinking in one dimension from which the quality of feeling has been excluded.

We talked about this a good deal at the symposium after Stephen Spender had read his paper, "Language As Communication," and at other times after Harold Rosenberg had introduced the views of Lionel Trilling about the hospitality the universities are now prepared to give to the arts. Spender's point was that language is the ultimate means of communication between the arts and sciences and among persons — "all human experience aspires to words. Yet," said Spender, "that fact is overlooked by the educators. Our own language is thought of as just one thing taught like all the others, not as intermediary between all things taught." English literature then becomes a subject, a specialization among other specializations, and "The main road of communication becomes a cellar occupied by people who make a profession of reading and writing."

This was a matter which worried us continually, whether we were talking about teachers or poets, novelists or painters-in-residence in the colleges and schools. They all run the hazard of being domesticated by the environment. Once the poet is in residence he is surrounded by professors in the English department, and, said Harold Rosenberg, "Before you know it, he begins to become a bit of a scholar; he begins to study not what he is interested in but what he thinks he ought to know, because whenever he goes to a cocktail party, someone is going to get him into a conversation about a minor historical item the poet doesn't know a damn thing about, but he thinks he has to go home and do his homework before he turns up again." "This is all true," said George Elliott. "Artists need other artists to talk to. You just plain have to have them — other people to fight with and agree with."

We were in general agreement that what was needed on the college and high school campuses was a sufficient number of artists and humanists of all kinds to make certain that the artist's point of view about art, not the academic's, could prevail and that the art itself, and not the talk about art, had to be the focus of interest. Harold Rosenberg told of a conference on art in education he had attended at which the members of the conference began referring to Matisse "as in Matisse," until he asked, "Why not put up a Matisse and talk about the painting?" The reply was that that was not necessary; "We're not ready for the work of art yet."

One of the difficulties in bringing the arts into the middle of the school and college culture is that the diffusion and dispersion of the creative artists away from their centers in New York, Paris, or San Francisco strips them of the opportunity to be with each other and to work in their own terms. Until there are enough of them in the educational institutions, we agreed that it would be a good idea to send teachers and artists from their institutions to New York for a year, or to London, or Paris, so that when they return to teach, they would have been close enough to the work now going on in the major art centers to be able to absorb it into their own teaching and creative work when they returned home.[3]

Another part of the solution lies in paying more attention to the young artists, performers, writers, composers, and dancers, already in the student body, giving them more time in the curriculum to work, and building up a community of interest in the arts as a whole so that the companionship of the visiting artists and the students can gradually develop into the equivalent of the world of the art centers themselves.

Throughout the symposium we kept returning to the central idea that there were in fact two worlds — the world of the artist and the world of the educators — and that the artists had to be continually on guard against being taken over, along with their art, and converted into useful instruments for mass culture and mass education. "There is a war on," said George Elliott, "between the mass culture and teachers and artists in the world who are trying to maintain and change those values which are being corrupted and destroyed by the mass media. It seems to me that

3. There is a program of this kind organized in connection with the Whitney Museum in New York for students, rather than teachers of art, who do studio work in painting and sculpture most of the time, visit galleries and museums, and attend a seminar once a week with art critics, painters, sculptors, and others. The New York Studio School has a similar program, run in collaboration with the students, most of whom have come from the colleges.

overwhelmingly, without any close second, the most important weapon we have is the accurate use of language. Just exactly that. Without that, only a very small elite audience is possible, an audience of a very small clique of writers and intellectuals. Anything like a general culture is impossible without first the plain, old-fashioned teaching of language. The textbooks are full of things that nobody would ever want to read. They are dreadfully bad reading in themselves. But the students are not required to write and to have their writing subjected to correction. Without this continuous discipline they will never learn, and do not in fact learn, to use the language. . . . The number of quite talented short story writers and poets who don't seem able to do what a good high school student should be able to do is considerable. I've read Ph.D. theses and M.A. theses which are disgraceful, written by English majors, disgracefully badly written. The corruption of language is very far advanced, very far indeed."

Harold Rosenberg strongly supported Elliott and Spender: "One of the big problems in painting and sculpture is the absence of the ability to communicate in words. There's a new kind of snobbery beginning to develop to eliminate language. Since people are illiterate, it isn't even necessary to learn to use words. . . . People say, 'Well, never mind about talk, about writing about art. We have the thing itself, the nonverbal form of communication.' The idea is that you'll be able to do away with words altogether. The fact of the matter is that a painting is so much involved with language in its conception and in its communication that any blow to words is a blow to all the other arts. I think what Spender says is absolutely of first importance. If people don't learn how to write better, everything will go down the drain."

It is also true that the talented teacher of English or American literature in the United States has become a major instrument through which the student in college can come in touch with what he needs to know about his own society and, to a certain extent, about himself. The teacher of literature has at his command a wide range of books, short stories, essays, poems, and plays, wider than ever before in the history of education and easily available through inexpensive mass-produced publications. In one sense the teacher of literature has taken the place of those teachers of philosophy of an earlier time who considered it their task to introduce questions of moral, religious, and social significance to their students, on the assumption that this was the responsibility of philosophy and of the teachers of philosophy. Now that the philosophers have abdicated that place in favor of presenting surveys of the history of philosophical systems or of problems in linguistic analysis, the vacuum has been filled by teachers of literature and the social sciences whose own intellectual interests take them into questions of philosophy and human values. They are already teaching the humanities under whatever labels their courses or department affiliations may be listed.

But no matter what else is done in the colleges, one central problem continues to plague the intellectual or the artist who is worried about the culture at large. The corruption of language goes on at a faster pace in the public discourse of television, advertising, and politics than anyone in the high schools and colleges can match by the counterforce of literature and the teaching of writing. Edgar Friedenberg pointed out in the discussion following Spender's paper that although he agreed completely with Spender's views, he did not think that any of the specific remedies proposed — more writing assignments for students, more and better teaching of literature, introducing the arts into the high school — could get to the center of the problem.

"We talk about this as if it were a consequence of something having gone wrong, or neglect, or people not doing what they know how to do, and we try to correct it as a physician might correct an illness in a patient. . . . This kind of abuse of language is a way of asserting, to use another quotation from Ortega, 'A commonplace mind, knowing itself to be commonplace, is asserting the rights of the commonplace and daring to proclaim it everywhere.' When an advertising writer writes with apostrophes, His 'n' Hers or Ship 'n' Shore, this is a way of saying that in this society you don't have to grow up. To complain about these things is right, but to set about naively to correct it is a little bit like complaining that the lethal chambers at San Quentin are poorly ventilated — you just don't understand what they're using it for. . . . What I'm saying is that it's not a matter of cleaning it up. It is that vulgarity is an active principle like *evil,* and so is sloppiness. It's an evil principle, but it isn't just a state of apathy."

We went on from there to talk about the way children seldom have a chance to express themselves freshly

and put it down to the fact that we have no oral tradition in expression which we honor and encourage inside
the educational system, because educators are more
interested in correctness than in imaginative expression, in speech, or in writing. Nancy Larrick and Maxine Greene pointed out that that was what was wrong
with the way children are taught to read and write,
and that most of the new and successful work going
on in the ghetto schools starts with the children talking about things they know and it advances from there
into written expression in poetry, stories, and children's
essays.

This brought up the question of bad writing by experts in science, journalism, and among scholars
and writers in general. Quite a lot was said about how
writers in the humanities simply leave to their editors
the job of making corrections to their bad writing. "In
some cases," said Stanley Kauffmann, "men of sub-
stantial intellect and learning assume that the development of their specialties frees them from the necessity
to learn how to express themselves in clear language."

Harold Rosenberg continued the point: "This may
be the most basic of all the problems — the profession-
alization of various forms of study and communication
that used to be part of literature. The arts are broken
down into subject specializations where each one develops his own jargon. In fact, I think the only way
that things become a speciality these days is to have
a jargon. Therefore a jargon is developed deliberately
to up the scale. This is happening in art criticism. People are trying very hard to develop a language no-

body would be able to understand. When this is accomplished, it will be possible to get a Ph.D. in art criticism. Now you can't do it because you don't know how to not say anything in the dubious manner that belongs to that profession. This will ultimately be accomplished, and so there will be another lump torn out of the English language. That's why I think it's perfectly true, as Friedenberg says, that there is a social basis for the destruction of language, and it may very well be that if you put English in the squeeze between the mass media on the one hand and the professional disciplines on the other, there's practically nothing left in the English language. It has been squeezed into a thin line."

Spender said: "I think there is quite a teaching point here which one knows from one's own practice. You were saying that bad writing comes from unclear thinking. But it is true that clear thinking comes from good writing, from improving one's writing. I notice often that one of the really blessed things about writing is that if you are confused about something but you want to express it, just write it, and then simply work at improving the language, simply work on the words, the grammar, and the rest, and then you can discover your own thoughts or you can discover whether your thoughts are worth anything."

I agree with this completely, and I think that it is another reason for thinking that an education in the humanities has to begin with an involvement of some kind by the student in the live materials of the sciences, the arts, and society, and that out of the involvement can then come some clarity about what it is the student thinks about the things he has experienced. For this reason I have always asked my students to write and talk about works of art, performances, social issues, and about the art they are themselves producing, for the reason Spender has given. Students begin to improvise a philosophy of art of their own by writing about performances they have seen; they begin to understand what the humanities are by forming their own judgments on questions raised by their own experience.

All this is only possible in a community where there are enough works of art being produced, presented, or performed, at whatever level of quality, to give people a chance to talk about them and write about them. In earlier years on the college campuses there weren't any art shows, or dance performances, or poetry readings, or new plays to talk about. The educational system did not include them. One of the reasons for the poverty of art criticism and theatre criticism around the country, in cities now possessing cultural centers and where performances and exhibits are fairly frequent, is that there is no place in the colleges for the development of writers who are themselves directly involved in the arts and no place to learn the art of criticism except by taking a job on a newspaper and covering performances and exhibits whenever they occur. There has been too little art and politics to write about on the campuses and too little chance for students to become interested enough in the arts and society either to become teachers of the arts or writers of criticism.

Charles Keller pointed out in the discussion that one of the reasons why there is so little chance for teachers to pay attention to the arts of language and criticism as a way of teaching students to think and feel is that high school English teachers are going full tilt, five classes a day, five days a week, and have no time to work with students on the quality of their writing. Neither do the students, since those going on to college are just as heavily scheduled in subject-matter areas as are the teachers, and the students not going on to college are assumed not to be interested, or in any case are not being educated to write well or to appreciate art, since theirs is a vocational and not a "cultural" future.

At the root of it all is the fact that the system grinds out graduates and the teachers are hired to do the grinding. The English department is hired to do the English, and the rest of the teachers think it is none of their business, even the teachers of the humanities. "There is too little interest in real teaching," said Keller. "The only thing you get out of good teaching is self-respect. You do not get promoted as a teacher."

What was said at the symposium confirmed most of the things I had found in my experience in the colleges and schools and in the reading I have done in the literature of education. I received specific confirmation on the matter of the condition of the present curriculum from a survey of the place of the humanities in American high schools,[4] carried out by Professor

---

4. Carolyn A. Glass and Richard I. Miller, "Humanities Courses in Secondary Schools," *Educational Theory*, July 1967, vol. 17, pp. 227-35.

Richard Miller of the College of Education of the University of Kentucky. Professor Miller prepared two questionnaires and sent one to the state departments of education and the other to institutions which offered work in the humanities. The state departments were asked three questions:

1. Were the departments publishing materials for the schools about the humanities?

Five of the states replied yes, 47 replied no, and two did not answer the question. The five states are Florida, Missouri, Pennsylvania, Puerto Rico, and Virginia. It is fair to deduce from this that by 1965 the state departments had not taken an active part in establishing humanities programs in their high schools.

2. Did the state department know of humanities programs in the schools of their states and, if so, which schools did they consider to be offering good courses in the field?

Thirty-one states answered yes, 20 replied no, and three indicated that they had no knowledge of such courses being taught in their states. Of the 31 states where courses are offered, most of them lie in the eastern half of the country, mainly in the northeastern section.

3. Could the departments give an estimate of the direction in which interest in the humanities is moving, particularly since 1960?

Thirty-seven answered "increased," 13 states answered "about the same," and four states made no indication. Another part of the question asked for the interest expected from 1965 to 1970. Forty-three states answered that an increase was expected, five replied "about the same," and six states gave no indication. Of the 31 states that replied yes to the question of whether humanities courses were being taught within their school systems, all noted an increase in the interest either at present or in the future.

Some reasons for the increased interest were given; for example, more attention is being paid to the needs of individual students, national publicity and conferences reflected new interests in the humanities in general, and a need to bring about a better balance in the present curriculum. While these reasons were dominant, others said that materials from the humanities were being read and discussed in greater measure as a result of Project English, a new emphasis upon literature and history was coupled with a tendency to identify the "educated man" as one who was familiar with the great books, and more school systems were now asking for information about the humanities. One state department replied that: "Apparently this is another of those cycles that education and society must go through. Usually it takes a decade to get it out of their system." In at least one state we can be certain that the baby will be thrown out with the bath water.

There are several things worth noting about the actual humanities courses which the schools reported. In the first place, the courses are to be found mainly in the larger schools, those having between 1,700 and 1,800 students where there is greater faculty specialization and more flexibility in the teaching programs. Since the questionnaire, in the form of its questions, assumed that the definition of the humanities had to do with course offerings in the fields of philosophy, history, art, or great books, it was natural that the replies would be put in those terms. The listing of course titles, for example, included: "Society and the Arts," "American Civilization," "Arts and Man," "Essential Ideas," and "History of Western Thought." For the majority of the schools, the humanities course is defined as a study of the allied arts or a combination of the allied arts, concepts, and philosophy. Most of the courses have been initiated since 1960.

A further analysis of the replies shows that only a small minority of the students were enrolled in the humanities courses. Usually the courses were electives for those going on to college and the students were juniors and seniors who were considered to be superior students. The courses were usually taught by English teachers; those in philosophy were usually taught by teachers who had taken a major in history or philosophy or had had some graduate or undergraduate work in philosophy. The Great Books teachers have usually taken English literature as their major field, and the average course in the humanities was taught by four teachers, most frequently with majors in English, art, music, history, or the social sciences.

According to Richard Miller, the obstacles to an expansion of the humanities curriculum consist mainly in the inadequate preparation of teachers, the fact that the high school curriculum is already jammed full with existing subjects, and that most teachers think of the humanities in terms of loosely related anthologies containing fragments of literature, philosophy, and social criticism. In those cases in which new work in the field could be identified as promising and relevant, teachers had made programs similar to those now being developed by the Educational Development Center in Newton, Massachusetts, where the main emphasis in constructing a new content is shown by titles such as "A Pilot Project in the Study of Mankind," "Myth and Art as Teaching Materials," and "Society and the Arts."

It is clear that to tinker with the curriculum, adding here, slicing there, or putting together "interdisciplinary" courses to get a "better balance" is simply to avoid the real problem, "To try," as Harold Rosenberg said at one point, "to put a grin on the face of this corpse." The real problem lies deep in social and cultural questions having to do with the development of modern American society. Our national goals, in education as elsewhere, are not being determined by the creative thinking and actions of statesmen, social scientists, philosophers, or educators but by the exigencies of short-term national reactions to national and international events in the flow of economic, political, and military history. To cite one instance, the country became interested in the science and mathematics curriculum in the high schools only after the Soviet space triumph had jolted the policy makers and the public into a state close to panic, even though it had been common knowledge among educators for years that that curriculum was grossly inadequate.

When the Second World War ended and the societies of the world fell into a new era, it was at first assumed that the role of the United States was one through which the ideas and programs of liberal democracy could be established on a world-wide scale. The hostility of the Soviet Union to those ideas and the mutual antagonisms between nation-states in a revolutionary period of world history moved the United States into a defensive posture, which it still maintains. The American educational system and the entire society were put to work to sustain a national goal of economic, political, and military security. That goal, which still dominates everything else, has badly damaged the ability of the American people to respond generously, imaginatively, and creatively to the reality of America's position in the world and to the circumstances of world politics.

The schools and universities have therefore become instruments of national policy rather than innovators of social change. In a culture dominated by mass media now used as tools to engineer various kinds of consent — in matters of taste and the consumption of products, in political ideology, foreign policy, cultural values — the educational system has seemed powerless to set in motion a flow of ideas and actions which could counteract the trend toward social and political conservatism. It is this phenomenon I see reflected in the curriculum of the American high school, and it is here that a major reform must begin, stretching back into the colleges and universities where teachers are prepared and into the political institutions which support them.

When national policy creates demands for more scientists and technologists, more soldiers, more managers, and more political conformity, the educational system bends to accommodate those demands, and the intellectual community is left with only its own demands for a larger share in making new policies of a different kind and with its own less powerful instruments for counteracting the trends in education that reflect the forces in the society. When we speak of the humanities, we are speaking of an area of concern where all social, moral, political, and cultural questions are raised in their greatest intensity and purity, and the duty of those who are involved in teaching American youth is to do everything possible to keep the level of intensity high in relation to those questions. This goes beyond an interest in the arts, taken by themselves, into an interest in the implications of political, cultural, and social decisions of all kinds and into the moral issues around which the values of the society form themselves.

On this point, Edgar Friedenberg's views as expressed at the symposium were quite explicit and altogether gloomy. He did not believe that much could be done about it all. Friedenberg said at the outset in his paper that he assumed his most useful function in the symposium would be to discuss: "How the schools are involved in humanistic education and how their limitations as social organisms set limits to what one may hope to undertake within them . . . and how the function of the school as a social institution determines, distorts, or limits the kind of artistic experience with which the school may deal and the ways in which it may, or may not, deal with it. The function of the schools," he continued, "is basically social and is carried out for the familiar reasons: to transmit the culture, promote social mobility, and assimilate youth of diverse backgrounds into a common American culture. These functions of the school have complemented each other in contributing to our historical development, but the effect they have jointly produced is antagonistic to, and probably cannot encompass, humanistic education."

The reason is that teachers and educators do not consider serious question-raising to be part of their duties, nor have they been educated in a way that would make it possible for them to do so in any case. Although the educational system has moved to the point that it now accepts the idea that the arts and humanities should be dealt with, either by participation in them or by learning something about them, "Involvement, authenticity, and passion are now the conventional insignia of the educated individual's approach to the arts and, as such, are frequently forged by students who wish to convince themselves or others that they are participating in a creative experience. This has become the appropriate, institutionally patterned way for a latter-day bourgeois to respond to the arts, and the schools teach it as part of the pattern of middle-class life. Leading students into this pattern of life and confining them in a middle-class conception of themselves are the central functions of the public school system. . . . To the degree that schools take the humanities seriously, they violate their preparatory function; for the arts are meaningful only as they comment on life as the artist actually knows it, and the comment is intelligible only to persons who have in some degree shared the experience and the social context of the artist. . . . The schools, engaged as they are in mass education, have neither the resources nor the inclination to examine any highly significant work thoroughly enough to be certain that its integrative power will be stronger than its disruptive force. When the curriculum committee considers including *The Assistant* on the reading list for English, the thing it can be sure of is that the Irish, the Jews, and the Flatbush Merchants' Association will all be insulted. Whether they will learn anything from it is more problematical."

Since Robert Shaw, Stephen Spender, George Elliott, Harold Rosenberg, and I had been arguing in our own nonsociological way that involvement in the arts themselves and an intensity of concern for the ideas and issues which emerged from a study of literary works could effect serious change in the quality of education in the schools, Friedenberg's paper and his comments on it brought a lot of things to a head. The paper itself, as is so much of what Friedenberg writes and as the reader who turns to it will note, was brilliant, and the thesis it argued was one familiar to those who have followed Friedenberg's work in research. But the hopelessness of its conclusions, and what some of us felt to be the over-inclusiveness of its sociological analysis, raised a series of responses in the symposium which, I think it is fair to say, put into question the validity of so completely sociological an interpretation of educational programs and institutions.

Certainly it is true that if the schools of the United States are to teach young Americans to enter their society with some talent for coping with it and some capacity for living in it usefully and fully, the schools need to pay attention to the arts and to the way in which students can learn about them. But because one pays attention to the arts and learns to know them, love them, and practice them, it cannot be assumed that the reason for doing so, either on the part of teachers or students, is to attract social approval and acquire a social asset.

When students become involved in acting in a play or writing one, or in discussing a moral issue or a work of art, they become involved in the thing itself. If, as a result, they are considered by others to have displayed a set of cultural interests and a knowledge of the arts and humane letters that is the mark of an educated person, this does not necessarily put them into the "pattern of middle-class life" or prove that their motive in becoming aesthetically and intellectually involved was simply to gain a higher social status. In fact, if the whole process works right, they are freed from the inverse snobbery of worrying about being considered middle class, or upper class for that matter, and they enter the classless world of the artist, where talent and interest are individually conceived, noted, and rewarded by a different kind of recognition. That is part of what the arts teach. What is needed is a strategy for education that can shift the emphasis away from the social rewards and approvals education provides and toward the fulfillment of individual talents and interests. Otherwise one simply enjoys the pessimism of a conviction that there is nothing to be done for students except to help them on their way to a prearranged doom.

Harold Rosenberg put his disagreement in a comment to Friedenberg in the discussion: "I completely agree with what you say, and I think you are absolutely right that these obstacles (to humanistic education) are there by design and not through lack of intelligence. We haven't brought up any ideas that are so new that somebody couldn't have thought of them fifty years ago. I think we should have started by saying: 'Is it utterly impossible to do anything? What *can* be done? What are the counterforces that would make it possible to do something in spite of the very solid existence of these conditions we are talking about?'"

Friedenberg replied that the prime function of persons interested in educational change of the kind we had been talking about was to make precise statements that are "authentic as well as cognitively precise about one's existential situation, in the light of all experience." His own experience had led Friedenberg to his conclusions, and a year spent interviewing students and teachers in high schools had persuaded him that, although there were occasional teachers who taught well there, the schools he visited were prisons, "some of them more comfortably decorated than others. . . . The teachers who were doing their jobs well I felt a combination of pity and terror for, but certainly any admiration that I felt had to be restricted to them and not extended generally to the enterprise with which they were associated. . . . You are ignoring the facts about what the social function of the schools really is and suggesting that that too is obsolete. The difficulty is that it isn't. That is to say that tying people together, obscuring their real differences, and sentimentalizing their experience are what made this country what it is today and are what holds it together. What I'm saying, in other words, is that the humanities, as I understand them, are essentially antifink and that the country is held together by a kind of institutionalized finkery. I'm not talking about the past, I'm talking about now."

It was suggested in reply that we would never know whether or not we could change the situation until we had at least put together a strong antifink platform and argued it publicly, which, in one sense, was what the symposium was trying to do. "In the case of insurmountable difficulties, you look to see if there is anything on your side at all," said Rosenberg. "It may very well be that there is not. We can, then, draw certain conclusions — that you might as well forget about the humanities altogether. . . . But if there is going to be a continuity between the arts and the world, in the things Robert Shaw and the rest of us have been talking about, it will be because certain individuals have picked up the banner and run with it until they dropped in their tracks. . . . We should look for the true obstacles. Instead of a conference on the humanities and the schools, there ought to be a conference on the obstacles to the humanities. Where do we get our ideas about what should be done in art in the schools? We talk to artists.

"Let's assume that what you [Friedenberg] say is so. I agree. All of us, more or less, as writers, have been operating on this assumption for many years. There are some alternatives. We simply have to look back to the past. . . . It was generally assumed that the arts had to be conducted outside of society if they were not to sink to the low level of thinking that the history of modern art is the history of bohemianism. It was simply taken for granted that there would be no use in an artist talking to you educators. It's as simple as that, and we therefore had no conferences. We had conferences, but not with you. Now we find that there has been a collapse of bohemia, and there is a new situation. It is also the fact that the universities have taken over to some degree a function that used to be the function of the outsiders — organized outsiders. That's what we should be talking about, how to make a common force within the university."

"We have to believe," said Spender, "that altering one school somewhere is going to alter something somewhere else."

Friedenberg agreed but pointed out that humanities and the arts acted as a kind of "detector organ" to discover what is wrong with the society. "It is the arts that tell you what is wrong, even though what is wrong is not primarily with the arts, fortunately, or the information would be more distorted than ever and that would make things even worse. But the fact that our contemporary painting, music, sculpture, and the rest are, by the standard or orderly tradition, as ugly as they are, is profoundly reassuring. That is, what is coming through the perceptive instrument is apparently valid. It's giving true testimony."

Rosenberg then said: "I want to agree with Friedenberg in regarding this as a process. I think that's the strong part of his position, and I'll back him up. As far as painting is concerned, we've had a whole wave of revolts. We've had very strong emotional expression, we've had what might be called ugly art. Now it's amazing how that same art becomes beautiful as soon as it reaches the institutions. This is what we are talking about. You take the presentation of contemporary American painting since the end of the War by the museums, and almost nothing of that art gets through. Once it leaves the studio, it is transformed into a force against it. This is the problem we are dealing with. It is not that you come up with a good idea and it will be adopted. That good idea is going to turn into another aspect of the same process. . . . There has to be an absolutely permanent revolt. The minute that art settles down into a good idea, that is the end of it.

"You have this same process going on in the colleges; that is, something good will happen, it will immediately become part of what we're objecting to, and then something else has to be done. For example, there is no question that painting and sculpture are being brought into the whole popular culture form of presentation. That is, they are becoming part of the entertainment world. The curator or the museum director is turning into the equivalent of a Hollywood producer. He's taking the work of the artist and making his own shows. That means that the shows are being made for the purposes of the institution, the institution is thinking of the turnstiles. . . . This is what is confronted by the artist in actual life, and it breeds in him a sense of despair in regard to his work. It makes the kind of work that expresses despair more significant than the kind of work that happily joins in this kind of presentation. When the work does happily join in, it becomes an adjunct of the mass culture product. That is what we are really talking about."

If we transpose what Rosenberg is saying in these comments into the situation of the universities, the parallel is exact, and although it does produce just as many gloomy problems as Friedenberg and the rest of us say it does, it also suggests that to call the problems gloomy is not to say that they are going to stay that way forever, or even if they do, that this is necessarily inhibiting to the possibilities of joy or aesthetic intensity. If the permanent revolt of the arts and artists is understood, accepted, and appreciated, then we add one more fact to the understanding of education and simply agree that as soon as a good idea is put to work in an institutional setting, it will be absorbed into one or another kind of institutional pattern and can then be attacked by critics simply because it is part of a new established order.

The point is that this is not an argument against putting up the good ideas or putting the arts into the schools and colleges. What the results will be is open to question, and it is important to remember that whatever the results may be, they *should* be questioned. It may be that radicals and liberals ask too much of society, that nothing we would get, in the purest of realizations, would be what we want, when what we should ask is that a society should provide a reasonably strong foundation on which many good things can happen as a result of the private aims and personal interests of a variety of people whose capacity to function creatively and fully is protected by the form of the society. In the rhetoric of the social philosopher, certain images of utopia have been passed into the vocabulary without sufficient attention to their validity, either as concepts or as desirable ends.

Even the metaphor, the "reconstruction of society," is a dated one, drawn from mechanical analogies of structures and forms that have too little relevance to the process by which societies actually change. We have seen in America in the last few years an infiltration of ideas from the artists, ideas that have loosened the grip of the cultural tradition and, therefore, of the political and social tradition. When things are said in novels, plays, films, and poems which express publicly what it has never been permissible to say, they break wide open the idea that there are in fact permanent authorities who have the right to decide what social and political norms are permissible. The role of the artist as the inventor of private *and* public truth can then be transposed by the citizen into his own life and into his relation with his government. What the educator can do is to create certain conditions of a pacifying and civilizing nature within the sphere of his influence in the institutions of society. Out of those conditions are created other conditions within which lie the possibilities of change, with the ultimate contribution of educators, artists, and humanistic scholars being that of making certain that we do not develop a hostile and violent society out of which no good can come.

Having been pressed into the issues involved in social change and education by the force of Friedenberg's argument, we talked our way out of it through something he said toward the end of the discussion of his paper. We had come around to the question of what individual teachers and institutions could do by way of starting counterforces and had settled on the idea that individual teachers did have responsibilities to recreate the system, as least as far as their own students were concerned. "Within the limits of the existing situation," said Friedenberg, "every year that I have been teaching — and I have never been nor ever wanted to be anything else — I struggle. I have become, I am sure, less charismatic, and hopefully so, more and more content to work with the relationships that establish themselves. In other words, I realize that the state is paying me to be of some service, as it works out, to perhaps eight per cent of the students enrolled in my classes. The others don't want anything I would regard it as legitimate to give; they want some other things that I generally try to make it possible for them to get, such as references to readings of a general character and someone to keep the record straight on them. But it doesn't bother me at all to feel that the fact that I am me and not somebody else matters to only a very small proportion of the students that I have to deal with. It also doesn't bother me at all, in fact I would be bothered if it were any other way, that I am personally unable to control, although I certainly can influence in terms of my own values, what the outcome of the relationship will be with those kids that I do have a relationship with and that I really like and can work with. I know perfectly well, nonetheless, that whatever I mean to them is not what

I meant to mean nor what I think I mean. But if I'm correct at least in its being a real relationship between two people, it will become, for better or for worse, a part of them."

Robert Shaw pointed out that if every teacher reached eight per cent of his students directly, this was a fairly high average, and that in his own teaching, if eight per cent were reached directly, this would mean that something had also happened to the other ninety-two per cent. "We have to believe, even if we do not have proof, that what we do helps everybody, and we would still have to go on teaching and believing in what we were doing. When people begin to sing and to play instruments, they are on their own; they have been taught what can be learned by way of expressing themselves in sound, and what they do with that expression is up to them. An art language," said Shaw, "whatever it might be, is so essential somehow to the nature of man that everybody has a little bit of it, and this is the place he can be touched most."

The issues around which the discussion turned then became an issue about the teacher and his intention and the relation between that intention and the stubborn resistance of masses of students and citizens whose interests and intentions are of a completely different kind from that of the teacher and the artist. If students come to college with a formidable disinterest in the arts and in questions of concern to artists and writers, it is possible that very little of what the teachers can do will turn the students in a different direction. On the other hand, it is possible to argue, and some of us did, that when students come to us with what are after all cultural, intellectual, and personal deficiencies, they are showing evidence of the pathology of cultural deprivation, and it is the responsibility of teachers and intellectuals to develop strategies of confrontation and reform through which the deficiences can be remedied. If we continue to think of students as the cultural proletariat, with the teachers and artists as an elite who have their own interests and talents which they are prepared to display in the students' presence, then we are taking no responsibility for changing the conditions of the culture but only for criticizing the conditions themselves.

Stanley Kauffmann in his paper had supported strongly the view that the duty of the teacher is to reach those who are reachable and to give to the rest the opportunity to discover whether or not they respond to the fine arts. "In this matter," said Kauffmann, "it is important to start with a clear, unsentimentalized view, free of democratic fallacies. A very small proportion of any country's population has at any time had a strong interest in art. I think it is a dangerous mistake to assume, as a dynamics in the teaching of humanities, that that proportion must be increased. If it happened to be increased, that would be lovely. What is more important is, first, that it be maintained, and second, that it be continually refined. . . .

"I am much more concerned with the touching of the few who will respond to art than with dabbing every member of the class with a little art veneer. . . . The chief safeguard against what we may call numerism is progressive, unpetrified elitism. Fine art is not for everybody, Tolstoy and his disciples notwithstanding. Democracy is a political theory, not an aesthetic one. Any teacher who is not an advocate of elitism, who does not approach the subject of art as the abbot of a religious order approaches novices — to find out which ones truly have the vocation, instead of trying to recruit them all — such a teacher is in my view a menace."

Harold Rosenberg agreed that it did not matter whether or not everyone became an artist. "I think what's important is that we have an enormous organized way of making use of human impulses in a partly unsatisfactory manner. . . . The art of our times has a double character. That is, the commercial forms of art are a double of art, they go along with it. They are the shadow, only the shadow is about a million times more powerful and solid than the reality. That's what we are dealing with. We are trying to replace the tremendous unreal enterprise with something that is more related to mankind. Instead of that reality we have these conventional forms of behavior in the arts. . . . Today everybody is involved in art. There is no person in the United States who in one way or another is not being given art training by television, by advertising, by the mass magazines. They are looking at Picassos in *Life* magazine . . . they are all in this culture. There is nobody outside of it, and we are talking about how you change that complex."

What it then came down to was the commitment of teachers to the nourishment and protection of the arts from the influences of the mass culture and that teachers, since they are also part of the mass culture and seldom have a chance in their preparation as teachers to come close to the reality of the arts themselves, were more likely to teach students proper behavior in the arts than to teach them to think and feel like artists. The circular effect on a system of teacher education that omits direct involvement in art and instead teaches "appreciation" in secondhand 'forms is then reinforced by the popular culture carried into the schools by the students and supported there by community values.

It seemed to me that to follow Stanley Kauffmann's reasoning would be to defeat the possibility that very much could be done to remedy this situation. If art is to have an effect only on the lives of those who are already capable of responding to it, teachers included, then two things follow: (1) it is being assumed that, contrary to the experience of a great many of us who have been teaching and educating for a long time, there are two kinds of students, those who can respond to the arts and those who cannot, and (2) that the effects of humanistic studies of all kinds are to be measured only by the degree to which the student has shown himself to be capable of a direct, continuing, and critical awareness of the arts themselves or shown himself to be capable of creative work of his own.

Although I am prepared to hear the word elite used without shuddering, I cannot accept elitism as a philosophy of education in any field or as a social philosophy capable of sustaining the aims of democracy. Kauffmann's emphasis on a clear, unsentimentalized view of art, free of democratic fallacies is one that recommends itself to all of us who are concerned with the place of the arts in a mass democracy. But when I consider the millions of children in the neglected areas of American society — in the urban and rural slums, in the cultural wasteland of the average middle-class public school — I find too close a connection between an elitist view of art and the hierarchical political philosophy of social classes to consider, unsentimentally, that art is a special enterprise of those who have a special gift for it.

Having seen the capacity of ignorant, uneducated, and culturally deprived children to respond to the kind of teaching which takes them where they are and calls upon the resources for aesthetic experience that lie within them, I must deny both on factual and theoretical grounds that the way to preserve the integrity of the arts and of the culture in which they are to flourish is by addressing the educators' attention to the talented ones, leaving the rest to get what they can. If this notion were applied to other sectors of the curriculum, we would then give up trying to teach children to read when they show no talent for it, and we would be satisfied never to raise the bigger issues of human life with anyone other than those who already know that such issues exist and must be dealt with.

In the discussion of the Kauffmann paper, the point was made that the film, which Stanley Kauffmann had identified as the newest and liveliest of all the arts, was a medium of art and value that could have the widest consequence in awakening the aesthetic interest of those unfamiliar with other forms of art or those who identified art as something to be appreciated by those in a separate cultural or social class. The familiar problem exists, of course, in developing standards of judgment and appreciation which go beyond the Hollywood and soap opera styles. But the film itself, when used as a medium for new works of art by student film-makers or as a source of imaginative teaching by those who take the trouble to select and present first-rate motion pictures to their students, either in class or as a class assignment, is a valuable instrument for dealing with the problem of arousing interest in serious works of art and serious human questions. Are those who see good movies only to be those who have already learned to seek them out?

We can take hope in the fact that already there are new forces stirring among students themselves, among many who are formally uneducated in the arts and the humanities but whose interest in the arts is actually derived from the mass culture. The rock musical, the idea of the mixed-media happening, the electric circus, and the folk-rock movement with its own poets and cultural heroes are derivations from popular culture through which a participant younger generation is creating its own art, good and bad. These are the forces of a new generation impatient with its elders and their art forms, prepared to protest, to invent, to take their own initiatives.

Theirs is a protest against the whole standardized pattern of American values and one which already starts with the sociological assumptions stated by Edgar Friedenberg, C. Wright Mills, Paul Goodman, David

Riesman, and others whose work has influenced the younger generation both consciously and unconsciously. The leaders of the protest movement see the standardized educational system as the main transmission agent of the system of middle-class values against which the older social critics so constantly inveigh. The young are writing their own poems, publishing their own underground magazines and newspapers, writing their own plays and acting in them, making their own films, composing and playing their own music, building their own curricula for the children of the poor, doing their own field research, and carrying out their own action programs in social change.

It remains for the educational system to adapt itself to the need reform-minded students are now expressing for more room to move and more relevance in their education, particularly as this is to be found in the humanistic studies and the social sciences. These students are the ones who should be entering the teaching profession, and until we go out to meet them, at least halfway, we are not going to get them there. I see no reason why, with the variety and wealth of talent in the arts and humanities displayed daily by the young generation, we do not do them the honor of including the interests of their present lives in the curricula of our schools and colleges. Students should not be forced to give up the arts and creative thinking simply because they enter an institution of education.

HAROLD ROSENBERG

Where to Begin

THIS IS MY FOURTH CONFERENCE on teaching art and my third on art teaching in primary and secondary schools. Through participation in these discussions I am beginning, I hope, to get an image of the subject a bit less blurred than it has been. I have begun to realize that art and art education are two different fields, or if you prefer, professions, and that, in practice, these professions have, ordinarily, nothing to do with each other.

An artist, an art historian, or an art critic asked to discuss the problem of teaching art thinks of how the student can be helped to become an artist or is one who understands what artists, past and present, have been doing.

He slowly discovers, however, that his view of the problem is fatally over-simplified. He has been focusing his attention on art as produced by people who have made it their vocation. But what does he know about the actual condition of the children in the grade schools to whom art is to be taught? Has he taken into account the competence of their teachers — and those who teach their teachers? Has he considered the qualifications set by state laws for obtaining a license to teach art in the public school system? What about the controllers of the school budget — and how do they feel about art? Has he considered what the public will accept? And the educators of the public, including the press and the mass media (who are, by the way, also in the art business and have their own aesthetic criteria)?

At the last conference I attended — a large, well financed, and very thoroughly prepared one — these issues were brought into the foreground by people who had been compelled to deal with them in their daily work. In the end they became the major considerations of art education. For instance, much attention was paid to the problem of primary, and even secondary, schools in which there was no teacher who had had any art training or in which there was a teacher who had happened to have three or four hours of art (whatever that means) in college. There were also questions of art rooms — or their absence, of the lack of art materials, of the indifference of parents to art or their hostility to it.

Every one of these problems is, obviously, of the utmost urgency in art education. I, personally, was so absorbed by them that it was only on the third day of the conference that I began to realize that what I had come to talk about, namely, the condition of art in

America at the present moment, and how, given this condition, it might be taught, was essentially irrelevant. An artist and an art historian who were also in attendance experienced the same sense of superfluity. The problems encountered by the educators were so real, and so full, rounded out, and complete that there was no room left for the difficulties of art.

In a kind of automatic, dreamlike way, we who had become, by contrast with the educators, representatives of the world of art, kept bringing up the topic of creating and appreciating art. Occasionally, one of us would rise to voice an objection when teaching art was made synonymous with teaching handicrafts, or with exercises in visual perception, or with the aesthetics of line, form, and color, or with inculcating rules of good taste in furniture, wall decoration, or fabric design. Each of us tried in his own way to recall that somewhere in the enterprise of teaching art the making of paintings and sculptures ought to be included, and that somewhere in teaching the appreciation of paintings and sculptures the ideas, feelings, and intentions of artists had to be taken into account.

The results of our efforts were not very encouraging. Most of the art educators, and particularly the educators of the educators, did not know, to put it bluntly, what we were talking about. Nor did they care. They had never learned much about art and had no time to think about it. They were specialists in education or in the psychology or philosophy of education. The few who had once painted or had studied art were pleased to hear echoes of the old art discussions and regarded us with the affectionate condescension reserved for those who express worthwhile truths but who are ignorant of the way things are in the real world. Others regarded us as trespassers in a field that belonged to them. The general feeling was: "Now we've had this talk about art, let's get down to business."

I, too, should like to get down to business.

There is no substitute art that can be taught simply because conditions make teaching art difficult or impossible. Teaching art means educating students, regardless of age, in the processes employed by artists in producing their works, in their attitudes toward their materials, in the character of *their* visual experience (not the visual-perception experiments of the psychologists), including their experience of works of art, and in the necessity for and the limits of imitation. The methods of teaching will, of course, be different in the kindergarten and in the art school, but the subject, as with ethics or religion, is the same whoever is being instructed. If there is no one in a school who knows anything of what artists do and think, art simply cannot be taught in that school. Someone may be found to distribute watercolor boxes and pans or to cut shapes out of colored paper for Halloween decorations, but there is no more reason why this should be called teaching art than exploding firecrackers should be called teaching chemistry. Art is culture, the culture developed by artists over millenia of creation. The subject matter of an art course, even in the lowest grades, is the artist and what he does and has done. It is not self-expression, or psychology of creation, or rules of how to match colors and harmonize forms.

Teaching false conceptions of what art is is worse than teaching nothing. It is preferable that children should get their art experience from toys and picture books, without a word about art, and that they should come upon art as they grow up and find themselves in the presence of art works, than that they should learn by rote certain experientially meaningless characteristics of masterpieces or be told that certain unexciting projects constitute making "art." The identification of art with "the finer things of life," that is to say, with the genteel, has for generations alienated from art the more vigorous minds in the classroom. The notion that art is unmanly, still fostered by approaching it in terms of taste and decoration, is one of the foundation stones of American anti-intellectualism.

To speak of teaching art in relation to art itself is, of course, to add a paramount difficulty to a situation already overloaded with difficulties. Perhaps it is the straw to break the camel's back. As I have indicated, however, it may well be that this particular camel's back ought to be broken. Certainly there is no sense in taking the existing art-teaching organism for granted. We should do better to look for new beginnings.

Let me repeat, the aim of art education is to bring the student into the orbit of art culture, either as a practitioner or as a participant in the experience of practitioners. Art education must function in proximity to the artist and the artist community. It must understand him and his part in the contemporary scene, for through him alone can it understand the arts and artists of the past.

Today, the coming together of the art teacher and the artist can be achieved only at the summit — that is to say, at the university. The suggestion is often made to bring artists into primary and secondary schools as teachers. Another suggestion is that these

schools make a systematic effort to reach out to painters and sculptors, if any, in their neighborhood or
community. These thoughts are in the right direction,
and perhaps a principal or teacher here and there
will take action on them. But local initiatives cannot
hope to produce any large changes in the life of art
in America and the manner in which it is taught.

If a new beginning is to be made, the key to it lies
with the university. This is especially the case today,
*when for the first time in our history the university
has become the training ground for artists as well as
for art teachers.* Those who are going to make art
and those who are going to educate people about it
are now studying side by side. This is a new situation,
and the more quickly its potentialities are recognized,
the better.

Until the 1950's it was the rule for American artists to
secure their training at professional art schools or by
working with older artists. Also, many were self-
taught. This practice has changed drastically in the
past decade. Today, the large majority of young American artists have attended universities and are holders
of academic degrees. Of the thirty American artists
under thirty-five included in the Whitney Museum's
"Young America 1965" exhibition, eighteen had B.A. or
B.F.A. degrees, six had attended college up to nine
years, five (of whom three had been born outside the
United States) had studied at art institutes (Chicago,
Boston, Rhode Island), and only one (also born abroad)
was self-taught.

The shift of art study to the universities is discussed by Lionel Trilling in the preface to his book,
Beyond Culture. Referring to Clark Kerr's concep-

tion of the university of the future as providing a favorable setting for "pure creative effort," Dr. Trilling comments that "Dr. Kerr's prophecy is but a reasonable projection into the future of a condition already established."

That art is not only being taught on the campus but being produced there provides a tremendous opportunity to develop a new kind of teacher — one who partakes directly of the experience which it will be his or her vocation to transmit. The art teacher who knows nothing about art reflects the physical separation that until recently existed between general education and the technical training of talented young people aiming at professional careers. There was in actuality no point of contact between teacher training and artist training. Now, however, the university has become a potential center of artistic creation and has made it possible for art creation and art teaching to develop together. This is another way of saying that the quality of art education in America will depend henceforth on how well art is taught in the university and how successfully artists are trained there, and this will be true on every level from the kindergarten to the studio. In sum, the university is the source from which must come not only the teachers in the primary and secondary schools, and the teachers of the teachers, but also the ideas and the programs and objectives by which these teachers will be guided either toward art or away from it.

The question, then, is: "How well fitted are the universities at present to stimulate the creative effort in art and art teaching referred to by Dr. Kerr?"

Dr. Trilling, in the book cited, notes that the new

role of the university in developing artists has been regarded by some with apprehension. There is dismay at the possible effects upon art of the large, impersonal institution and the academic approach. In Dr. Trilling's opinion these fears are groundless. Within the past thirty years, he believes, American universities have been freed of their otherworldliness and have entered into a happy relationship with the arts. Once a "citadel of conservatism, even of reaction," Dr. Trilling observes, today "nothing in life is so mundane and practical or so rarified and strange that the university will not take it into sympathetic consideration."

Perhaps Dr. Trilling is right about the imaginativeness of universities. But I wonder if their "sympathy" carries over into practice. My suspicion is that while liberalism is the prevailing doctrine in the university theory, administrative officers enforce codes rather than ponder individual idiosyncrasies. But even if Dr. Trilling is right in his estimate of what might be acceptable, hospitality to oddness or intransigence is hardly of itself a sufficient foundation for the growth of the creative mind. Certain characteristics inherent in the university situation present serious drawbacks to achieving good results in the arts by both students and faculty. In individual cases — and creation is always an individual case — these drawbacks, or any one of them, can be fatal.

Four major weaknesses in the university situation as it affects the development of an authentic art consciousness come quickly to mind:

1. The need to turn art into a teachable subject in which the effort applied will produce predictable re-

sults, such as are obtained in other studies.

In creation, of course, nothing is predictable. An artist may strive diligently along indicated lines and achieve only mediocre results. Then a mistake leads to a discovery, an accident to a new start, a near-fatal illness to a rebirth and vision, etc.

Art, however, is not only creation. It is also skill and technique in handling materials, whether words, sentences, and paragraphs, or color, line, and form. In these aspects of art, results *are* predictable, at least sufficiently so to make possible the allocation of grades and certificates attesting to a quantity of work satisfactorily completed.

The need of the university art department (or, for that matter, the creative writing department) to regularize the teaching of its subject leads it to assume automatically that attitude toward the arts which stresses their craft aspects. Masterpieces are analyzed as if they were triumphs in the application of skills. Both the cultural setting of the artist and the individual quality of his performance are put aside, while his work is praised in terms that would have earned him an "A" in a woodworking course.

Today, the craft approach to art is reactionary and out of touch with the actual modes and functions of twentieth-century art. In the past a student could be introduced to the national or regional tradition by learning studio or workshop procedures. In our time art is involved with ideas; it is a creation of the mind as well as of the hand. In order to deal with living art, the university must find the means to overcome the drift toward reducing art to a system of measurable skills.

2. A second weakness is lack of knowledge of the creative situation and misinterpretation of the content of existing art.

For all the current open-mindedness toward the rebel and the eccentric, there is very little teaching of the radical intellectual and imaginative content of the art of this century. Generally, the history of contemporary art is covered in a superficial survey, and the tendency is to present it in a vocabulary that amalgamates it into the evolution of certain formal values, or of man's power to represent nature, which presumably constitute the ideals of art in all ages. Specific responses of artists to their time, place, and cultural situation, including their negative responses to both art and society, are filtered out of the works for the sake of an orderly arrangement within the history of forms. Thus the student learns about some obscure activity called art, the products of which people treasure and deal in as they do gems or old coins. He does not gain an experience of art or a glimpse of his world as seen by artists.

When no connection is established between art and life, the problems of teaching art are multiplied, especially of teaching it in the primary and secondary schools. Modern art is deeply related to the feelings of strangeness and revolt felt by children, particularly those children who may be most resistant to the classroom. Often the delinquent or the dropout is one step from art, as was successfully demonstrated by the High School for the Performing Arts in New York. If art were presented in terms of its actual daily life, many problems of arousing student interest would simply vanish.

3. Another weakness is physical dispersion. The artist or the art major in the university is cut off from direct contact with developments in the larger art centers. Moreover, he is isolated among specialists in many different fields.

The university artist or art teacher receives news of the work being done and the ideas being discussed in New York, Los Angeles, or Chicago only sporadically and at secondhand. He does not himself participate in the daily life in which new trends are developed, new problems raised, new possibilities explored. To hold his own in the academic environment he begins to regard himself too as a specialist and devotes himself to the acquisition of information rather than to the exploration of his own mind and evaluation of trends in his medium.

How destructive to both art and art education this isolation from current creation can be is indicated by recent developments in American poetry and fiction. With writers spotted around the country in university posts, not only has imaginative writing been overwhelmed by criticism, but criticism in turn has tended to lose touch with literature and to revolve around its own rules, assumptions, and procedures.

4. A final problem is diffusion of thought, attention, and effort.

Art majors are kept from fully pursuing their interest in the springtide of their enthusiasm by requirements of the liberal arts courses. It goes without saying that the artist-in-training and the teacher-in-training should secure the broadest possible general education. But this education need not be unrelated to his work in the studio or study of the art of the past. The history of art is the history of its relation to religion, philosophy, mathematics, politics, biology, fashion, social history, psychology — more than enough topics to constitute a full academic education. The study of these subjects, if presented in the perspective of the student's art studies, would immeasurably enrich his art experience rather than tending to blot it out. At the same time it would make those subjects themselves more vital and meaningful.

These problems of the university in its relation to the creative mind cannot be overcome by mere official sympathy for what Dr. Trilling calls the "rarified and strange." The creative life is not easily made compatible with a large, well-functioning institution attentive to other interests. Creation involves, for instance, confusion and waste of time. It transvaluates values, flouts or even attacks what seems self-evident to the majority.

Mr. Emerson Andrews, the nation's leading authority on foundation giving, has said that giving in the creative arts is the most difficult form of philanthropy, since it must itself be an act of creation, demanding conviction, courage, and a willingness to assume risks.

In the university the problems of the foundation are magnified. Not only does the university have to expend funds on this undefinable objective called the creative, it must assume, too, responsibility for the physical charge of young people and justify to parents and the public its contribution in exposing them to the hazards of creation.

Given these weaknesses and dilemmas at the university source of our art energies, what improvement may we expect in art work in the primary and secondary schools? The answer is, obviously, not much.

New devices, techniques, expenditures, programs, teaching machines will not avail in the absence of creatively motivated people, genuinely educated in art.

What is needed above all is a new attitude or, one might say, a philosophy — the philosophy of looking to art itself for clues as to what to do and what to teach. The art of the past hundred years is a vast continent of experience in both the creation of art and in the intellectual appropriation of the art of the past. Today this continent lies virtually unexplored. Yet here alone is the ground on which can be built that community of creation out of which genuine art education must come.

For art to become, as the declaration of purpose of this symposium states, "a more central and invigorating part of the curriculum of primary and secondary schools," it must commence by becoming a more central and invigorating part of the minds of our intellectual leaders. Our educators, both in schools and out of them, have been all too generous in devoting their intellectual resources to proposing means for instructing the ignorant, whether children or adults. They have been less concerned with educating themselves, with raising their thinking to the level of the cultural realities of the age. The first lag to be overcome is the lag at the top. Perhaps our discussing what art is today and what it is for is not irrelevant to primary and secondary school education after all. It may well be that the chief message which art brings to education at any age is that it is impossible to teach unless the teacher is in the process of learning.

STEPHEN SPENDER

Language as Communication

In the famous controversy about the two cultures, one important point seems to have been overlooked — that if there truly is a gulf between the literary and the scientific culture, this cannot be bridged by science but only by language. Language is the only means of communication between specialties as far apart as every individual's unique experience of his own life. Scientific specialization itself is human experience; if it is to become part of the general culture, it can only be so by communication through language. When there is a question of discussing and explaining our experiences of the other arts — music or painting — we use words. If architecture aspires to the condition of music, all human experience aspires to words.

This very simple point, that we communicate by means of language, seems to be largely overlooked by our educators. Our own language is thought of as just one thing taught like all the others, not as intermediary between all things taught. Before the end of the last century, English, I believe, was not a subject at English universities; there was no English school at Oxford or Cambridge. Everyone was supposed to know English literature, and apart from the grammar taught in one's childhood, how to write English was a benefit conferred by, or inferred from, a classical education. I suppose that some of those who hotly contested the introduction of the study of English literature must have argued, with reason, that if English becomes a subject, then reading and writing English literature becomes a specialization among other specializations. The main road of communication becomes a cellar occupied by people who make a profession of reading and writing.

In our own time an attempt is being made to turn the tables on those who have made English one subject among other subjects by giving it the status of principal subject. Dr. Leavis and his followers argue that English should be the main study at the new universities. They argue that in the era of the breakdown of values, and in the absence of religion, our only connection with the past of the "organic community" is through the English books of the Great Tradition, as chosen by the Leavisite priesthood.

This seems an attempt to replace compulsory religious teaching with compulsory study of English literature. It seems an extreme position only serving to dramatize that it is a desperate one in the age of nuclear fission when the people who are studying either to reinvent us or to completely destroy us, have no time for any other work than their frenetic pursuit of bigger and better means of doing one or the other.

What one may insist on, though, is that life attains significance through the consciousness of the individual who lives it and who is able to understand that significance through comparing his own experiences with those of other people. Language is the only means of communicating experiences, realizing consciousness. One cannot, I think, reasonably argue that everyone ought to be a new critic or a doctrinaire of the Great Tradition, but one can point out that it is urgent for people to be able to communicate, and that they can only do this through being able to read works which illuminate their lives; and this means developing a capacity to speak, think, and write clearly.

It seems to be universally recognized that everyone should learn to read and write. Not to be able to do so is to be illiterate. Little importance, however, is attached to *what* you read and how you write. The idea that writing is not just a physical attainment, like using a knife and fork, but is communication, and that everyone should be concerned with it to the degree that he has experiences and ideas to express seems to be regarded as eccentric. Yet it is doubtful whether you can carry on an intelligent conversation without being able to write down the ideas conversed about. Anyone can demonstrate this to himself by simply turning on the radio or TV and listening to the dismal attempts of experts in politics and government to communicate their expertise. What one witnesses again and again is the breakdown of language.

We groan over specialization, but we accept it as inevitable, reflecting that specialists are specialized in matters of which we are so ignorant that even if they could tell us about the things they know, we would not understand. Yet there exist, especially in France and England, a few masters of exposition who show that the most specialized subject is often far more communicable than we would expect it to be. Moreover, it is doubtful whether what we need or want to know from the specialist is really that which is highly technical and particular to his research. What we need to know from scientists is how their scientific picture of the world should affect and qualify our own general picture, in fact, our consciousness of life. A good deal of this *can* be explained. And if — as Robert Oppenheimer seemed to think — there is a highly important kind of scientific experience which cannot be communicated to the nonspecialist, then the significance of noncommunicability is something which also needs to be explained, because it may be a factor, or rather, a blank, in the picture of life which we need to allow for. In the past it was considered important to understand that there were incommunicable mysteries. But these were communicated partly in the sense that people knew what kinds of experience they were about. In the same way, the significance of the incommunicability of some areas of science is something we need to understand.

Whether what scientists have to explain to us is communicable, or whether they have to explain that it is incommunicable, the fact is that the present breakdown in communication is due at least partly to the neglect of English. It is slovenly to accept without question the idea that we cannot communicate because of our age of specialization. One only has to look at the essays of most sociologists to realize that language, the medium of communication, is often the last thing that people who have very important things to tell about the state of our society have taken trouble about. We enter the era of mass communication when the study of the traditional, and the ultimate, means of communication, the English language, is looked at as a matter concerning only literary specialists.

I do not see why an attempt should not be made at school, through the widened study of writing and speaking English, to break down some barriers of in-communicability. The basic condition for making such an attempt possible would be that everyone, in what-ever discipline, wrote an essay on some general subject once a week or fortnight. Some of these essays might take the form of communications from members of one discipline to another. For example, students on the science side of the school might be asked to write essays directed to those studying history, explaining, in words the science student hopes the historian would understand, what some aspect of his science was "about," and vice versa. The historians, or the scientists, would then read the best essays from the science students, and perhaps both classes would meet to discuss the essays.

Another exercise I have thought about (without my being able to fire anyone else with my own enthusiasm) is that a day of a term or a year should be set aside for a general academic exercise in which speakers from different specialized disciplines would explain before an audience what they thought was the meaning and importance of their work.

I think, then, that we should regard English litera-ture — fiction, nonfiction, poetry, and the rest — primar-

ily as teaching people to communicate with one another and, in that way, helping them to live their
lives. We are not, at the level of school or even at that
of the university creative writing course, teaching them
to be writers. We are concerned only with teaching
them to read, to express themselves, to appreciate language, and to discuss and talk better because they are
trying to read and write. Instead of giving them a
specialist view of writing, we should try to break this
down, to emphasize the importance of writing everything as well as possible — a letter to a friend or family
or a private journal. We should make them think of
reading and writing as two sides of the same medal —
one reads better because one writes better; one writes
better because one reads better.

That students often distinguish sharply between
reading and writing is painfully evident. Some years
ago, after reading an essay by one of my students, I
suggested to her that she should read Samuel Butler's
essays. "Oh, I don't read, Mr. Spender," she protested,
"I write."

As I suggested above, every student at school ought
to write a weekly essay. Students ought to be given a
wide choice of subjects, with a view perhaps to their
sometimes being very close to themselves and sometimes demanding that they should get away from their
self-absorption and their subjectivity into their opposite, the objective. I am in favor of their writing, occasionally, the Charles Lamb type of essay on "Roast-
ing a Pig," or "Moonlit Apples." But it is a mistake to
produce the impression that this kind of *belles lettres*
is literature or, at any rate, more literary than the
subject I suggested previously of a scientist writing for

a historian about his scientific studies. Everything that is well written can be literature, if literature is what we are concerned with. One of the English master-pieces is a handbook on angling.

Feeling for language includes grammar, texture of sentences, the difference between prose and poetry. The important thing is to emphasize the sensuous aspects of writing. For example, grammar is not just obeying rules. It is the exercise of the power politics of language. Words rule other words; subjects have objects; prepositions are powerful indicators, instruments of authority, traffic directors. All this suggests the visual, and it seems to me that grammar should be visualized as much as possible, with parentheses enclosed in separating walls, nouns elevated to kingship by verbs and ruling their objects, and so on.

I hope the following poem of mine will illustrate what I am here trying to put forward:

"Subject: Object: Sentence"
A subject thought: because he had a verb
With several objects, that he ruled a sentence.
Had not Grammar willed him these substantives
Which he came into, as his just inheritance?

His objects were *wine, women, fame* and *wealth,*
And a subordinate clause — *all life can give.*
He grew so fond of having these that, finally,
He found himself becoming quite subjective.

Subject, the dictionary warned, means *someone ruled by*
Person or thing. Was he not *having's* slave?

To achieve detachment, he must be *objective*
Which meant to free himself from the verb *have*.

Seeking detachment, he studied the context
Around his sentence, to place it in perspective:
Paraphrased, he made a critical analysis,
And then reread it, feeling more *objective*.

Then, with a shock, he realized that *sentence*
Like *subject-object*, is treacherously double.
A sentence is condemned to stay as stated —
As in *life-sentence, death-sentence*, for example.

Apart from one term teaching school in England, most of my experience of teaching is in a creative writing course at Northwestern University — an "advanced composition course" as we call it there. Before discussing this I feel the need to make an apologia, to explain what my attitude is to such a course. Most writers feel, I gather, the same need to justify teaching "creative writing."

I do not think that the writer teaching such a course thinks that he can provide a formula which will turn students into poets and novelists. A writing course sets up a meeting place for students who are interested in writing. Here they exchange views and come in contact with a vocational writer. The creative writing course is a midwestern substitute for the Parisian café, where young writers come and show one another their poems and stories, and where older writers are in the offing. The more students, with or without the official "writer," meet and continue their discussions outside the course, the better. I am very doubtful whether I have been of much help to the potential writers in my courses. I do think, though, that the atmosphere of a community has been created quite early in the course, and that this has been helpful.

The most difficult thing to teach writer-students is how to approach the problem of writing poetry. Obviously what one can do is give them an idea of the techniques of prosody, of the forms in which poems have been written, and of different metrical patterns. I understand that W. H. Auden, when he taught a course at Ann Arbor, concentrated very much on technique. He would make his students write sonnets, sestinas, etc. Parenthetically, it is worth noting as a matter of literary history that the presence of Auden in America has — at any rate until quite recently — enormously stimulated the interest of young Americans in writing poems in traditional forms.

To my mind, teaching poets to write in a wide variety of forms has its dangers. For a good many professional poets, especially among the moderns, have got on very well without knowing any more about form than was necessary to them for writing their own kind of poetry. A poet may not need to know more about form than suits his purposes at a particular stage of his development; continuing beyond this stage he acquires new techniques when they are needed. To a poet who has read a good deal of poetry by other poets, form — the kind of form he needs for his own development — may come almost instinctively. When Auden was an undergraduate and started writing his own early poetry, he read a great deal but he had very little theoretical knowledge of form. The forms of his earlier work are more or less instinctive echoes of

Anglo-Saxon, Hardy, "The Waste Land," and "The Tower" of W. B. Yeats. Only about five years later did he seriously study a great many forms and become a virtuoso in them.

Another example which illustrates my doubt as to whether students should write exercises in traditional forms in poetry is from Robert Graves. Graves rarely if ever writes poems in which he shows interest in the virtuosity of form. Reading his poems one has the impression that his stanza patterns "come" to him. I once asked him about this, and he explained that the first lines of a poem nearly always came into his head in a certain pattern, and then, when writing the poem, he simply followed the stanza pattern throughout. I asked him what he did if he found that the accidental-seeming stanza pattern did not work — did he then begin from the beginning of the poem, in a new pattern? He said, no, if this happened he simply scrapped the poem.

Again, rereading recently T. S. Eliot's 1917 essay on the technique of Ezra Pound, it struck me that the young Eliot applied remarkably little formal analysis to the work of Pound who, at that time, was open to such analysis, since he then often wrote poems in conventional forms. Eliot writes not of "form" but of "technique," by which he means something different — the ability of the poet to create a language which is absolutely true to the music of his own ear, to the inner rhythms of his mind.

Another scruple of the same kind is my feeling that it might have been a positive disadvantage to Walt Whitman to have known how to write a sestina or a sonnet. Whitman was more made by what he did not know than by what he knew.

So I have doubts about teaching students to do exercises in a variety of conventional forms. Formal writing tends to become a habit which may not serve the interests of the writer's true development, and then it becomes difficult to shake off. Yet it may be argued that in teaching poetry — an unteachable subject about which, nonetheless, a lot can be learned — you have to make it "academic" for it to be a subject at all. Some students gain from doing academic exercises.

Perhaps one should divide students into groups of those who can gain from using conventional forms and of those who stand to lose by it. The imagists, within their narrow limits, were the only true modern poetic "schools" in English (in France, Mallarmé, and Laforgue may have been another) in the sense of teaching poetry. What they taught was that the poet must create an image in language which is true to a "real" image, and which is realized with concreteness and the utmost economy, without regard for music and conventional form. Pound taught poetry by reduction of its aims to a minimum which can be taught.

There are, in general, a few learnable things about writing poetry: for example, to be careful about the consistency and concreteness of metaphors, to reduce adjectives to a minimum, to avoid archaisms, to realize that there is a certain literalness in poetry about the action of prepositions ("through" in a poem is like a line drawn through the diameter of a circle). Also the student can be taught to avoid being intoxicated by his emotions about other poets (e.g., about Ginsberg) and to look carefully at those poems which, of their kind, are models (e.g., Robert Graves, and some of Auden).

Having instilled a little discipline into some students, perhaps others can be taught something by one attempting to loosen up their imaginations, through free association and surrealist games. I have always thought that it would be a good idea to encourage each student to write for class at least one thoroughly erotic poem. Lastly the teacher can use himself as a guinea pig for the benefit of the class, describing his own approach to writing poetry, and illustrating the development of a poem from his own sketches.

I have heard that Auden made his students at Michigan learn by heart a canto of Dante in the Italian without regard to whether or not they knew the language. This sounds zany, but it might be inspired. Without knowing Italian, the student can get enough hang of the language to see the crystalline qualities of Dante, the greatest of all teachers of other poets. To look at a poem in another language is a way of seeing — projected as it were onto a screen — how the unfamiliar words work. One is too involved with one's own language to have the same sense of the pure function of words as poetry in it, as one may get from Italian, French, German, or Latin. Artistic effects appear more deliberate in a language not one's own. And deliberation is all that can be taught, spontaneity has to come of its own.

The most difficult thing in teaching an art is to make a student recognize his mistakes. This is no doubt partly due to the confusion of standards today, which may result in the student genuinely writing, or going through the act of writing, according to standards quite different from those the teacher brings to bear on his work. But there is in America today a type of student who seems to write poems as though they are briefs to be defended in a court of law. He justifies what he has not expressed by explaining at length what he intended to express, and why he thinks it is there. This makes teaching extremely difficult because the most important of all things for an artist to know is where he has gone wrong. What the teacher really has to contest is the student's idea that writing is just a lottery — you put down something and maybe someone else will think it is marvelous. Or you wanted to say something and it is only ill will on the part of others which makes them refuse to see that you have said it. Once I received the following letter from a student: "Dear Mr. S., I was just about to throw these poems away when it occurred to me that *you* might like them." So he enclosed two hundred pages of manuscript.

Possibly these experiences of teaching creative writing will seem too advanced for schools. But they may suggest an attitude toward teaching English in school which could be helpful. This is to draw attention to language as an instrument, by comparing the different uses to which language is put in poetry and prose. Students are intrigued by questions such as: "What is poetry?" "What is the difference between poetry and prose?" One may point out to them that the answers to these questions are not absolute. There is no line completely dividing some poetry from some prose, some prose from some poetry. The difference between poetry and prose lies in the kind of use to which language is put, the direction in which it is being made to move. Prose directs language in one way, poetry in another. We get the feel of the difference between prose and poetry from the pull, the tug of language in one or the other direction, rather than from language arriving at a prose or a poetry goal.

In the prose use of language the words used tend to disappear into the object — of nature, of events, of ideas, or persons conveyed, so that the reader is left with the object (scenery, a love affair, the categorical imperative, M. Charlus) without the particular verbal formula in which it was conveyed. With poetry there is the opposite tendency. The object tends to disappear into, to become replaced by, the words, which become verbal objects. We do not think of the nightingale in Keats's ode as something having a life independent of the words used by Keats. On the contrary, the function of the "dryad of the trees" is to bring us back perpetually to the words, so that we cannot even begin to think about anything in the poem without thinking of the words. The poet sets experiences and words chasing one another in a vicious circle, a *perpetuum mobile*.

Everybody does not have to like poetry. This is a truism, but it is not obvious to some enthusiastic teachers who seem to regard poetry as a crusade. In order to write or read and enjoy poetry you have to take a sensuous pleasure in words for their own sake, and not regard them as mere conveyors of a sense which can be replaced by other words. Rather few people enjoy words for their own sake, and though something can be done to stimulate such enjoyment (perhaps discussion of words themselves, interest encouraged in dictionaries, the use of Roget's *Thesaurus,* etc.), some students will resist poetry. They may even do so because they have a passion for accurate prose, exact language disappearing into the objects described. It would be wrong to be snobbish about this, and to risk putting the student off literature forever simply because he does not like poetry.

People who do like poetry find in it such significance that they are tempted to think that poetry nonlovers scarcely live their lives. For the poet, everything significant has poetic significance, and consequently whatever does not have poetic significance seems to him routine, material, at best the potential stuff for a future poetry.

The essentially cultist attitude is deplorable at all times, but it should specially be kept out of education. What is vitally important in education is that people should communicate, that they should develop to the greatest extent their awareness of themselves and of others, that they should learn to have contact with the life and the values of the past enclosed in masterpieces, with the same freedom as they might speak to a wholly articulate and vividly alive friend or neighbor. Language is the lifeline between person and person, contemporaries and the past. Teachers of English therefore have an immense responsibility because they help a young generation make consciousness articulate.

STANLEY KAUFMANN

Films and the Future

I BEGIN WITH COMMENTS on an occasion that I think is directly related to the subject of this meeting — the opening of the new Lincoln Center Repertory Theatre in 1965 with a production of *Danton's Death*. Those of you who are interested in these matters may have read that the company in fact started in 1963 in a temporary building and was generally coolly received, that its then management, of successful Broadway types, was roundly disapproved by most serious critics, that the appointment of a new management — Blau and Irving of the San Francisco Actors' Workshop — was generally hailed. I was among the hailers because, although I had never seen a Workshop production, I knew the plays they had been doing, the atmosphere they had created, and that Blau and Irving had gained their reputations by turning their backs on what the com-

Copyright © 1968 by Stanley Kauffmann

mercial theatre signifies. Then came the first Blau-Irving production in New York. One cannot, of course, reach final decisions about them or about the future growth of the company on the basis of one production, but this time, as against the first management's productions, there was a feeling not of rage but of hopelessness. *Danton's Death* was poorly produced in every regard, and I felt that I was facing, not Broadway slicked-up superficial art, but an exponent of American bankruptcy in the performing arts, that the poverty on the stage was *our* poverty, that that stage was a combination mirror and magnifying glass.

Or to take another instance that leads back to the subject of this meeting, Federico Fellini, the Italian film director, was in New York recently, and in conversation he said: "I have been in New York five or six times, and each time it seems to me made up of pieces of dreams I had when I was a boy. Why have I never seen New York rightly used in an American film? And where are the good new American films altogether?"

I replied, not entirely evasively, that the answer would entail a concise restatement of American history — and not just its cultural history. So instead, I asked him to have another drink.

These two instances are not meant as glib evidence that this country is bankrupt of artistic talent, because it most certainly is not. But I'm here specifically as a commentator on the theatre and on films, and these two arts are at present in especially poor estate in contrast to several other American arts; and since these two arts are most clearly related to large audiences, their condition seems to me to reflect mercilessly the condition of the American public; this, by easy progress, this relates to the education, expectancies, appetites of that public.

I'd like now to state my conclusion to make clear what I'm progressing toward. It is simply this — art of any kind is a circular process. It is obviously not made without artists; less obviously, but equally pertinently, it is not made, for long or well, without a responsive audience. Talent is a relative constant in the human race; it flowers when there is the right public soil. We all know of individual exceptions to this, artists who worked all their lives, unaccepted and unknown; but they are exceptions. The great eras in any art — painting, music, poetry, architecture, drama — were sustained by appetites in a society. The elements that produce that appetite are many and are tightly interwoven — political, economic, religious, the home, the school. None of them can, rationally, be entirely isolated from the others. But, recognizing the irrationality, we can discuss what teachers can do with young people to improve appetites for art in this country's future.

In this matter it is important to start with a clear, unsentimentalized view, free of democratic fallacies. A very small proportion of any country's population has at any time had a strong interest in art. I think it is a dangerous mistake to assume, as a dynamics in the teaching of humanities, that that proportion must be increased. If it happened to be increased, that would be lovely. What is much more important is, first, that it be maintained, and second, that it be continually refined.

The aims of the teacher and the hopes of the critic are not necessarily identical. The teacher presumably wants to send out every pupil more of a whole-souled being than he was when he came in. Theoretically, at least, he has equal responsibility to every pupil, to enlighten the pupil to the best of both their abilities in the subject he teaches, in the time and at the stage that their meeting takes place. As a citizen, I applaud; as a critic, I don't much care. That is, I am much more concerned with touching the few who will respond to the art than with dabbing every member of the class with a little art veneer. Of course one cannot reliably know in advance who the responsive few will be, and therefore the approach must be to the whole class. What I am concerned with is the *intent* of the approach, so that when those few are reached, they are given help instead of — as often happens — hindrance that may take years to overcome. It is culturally more important that those few get some glimmer of the mysteries and uncertainties of art than that the majority be given a few facile certainties to make them feel they have a grip on the subject. When I was in grammar school and high school, music appreciation exams consisted of the teacher playing brief snatches on the phonograph and asking us to write down the name of the composer and the title of the piece. It bred a good number of graduates who felt that the ability to name the composer and title was the mark of the musical connoisseur.

I am not going to discuss here the subject of awakening latent creative artistic ability in students. That can happen and does happen, but it is necessarily much rarer than this matter of cultivating a demanding audience. Anyway, it follows, both socially and educatively, if that audience is properly cultivated.

Thus my view of the teaching of the arts is that it ought never to be construed as in any way a parallel to the teaching of arithmetic or reading or geography, of which everyone must know something. It is not necessary — to the individual or to society — that every individual feels some link or responsibility to fine art; that concept is delusory, fallacious, and corrosive. It *is* important that every student be given a chance to find out whether he responds to fine art. I should judge that the only way to grade this approach is in terms of the student's age, what his experience of life and his possible imaginative reach may be. Within that framework, nothing but the best should be given him — in materials or in guidance. The former is relatively easy to give him, the latter less so.

This decade is one of insistent cultural explosion. The explosion has so far been largely in terms of the measurable, producible, and controllable: the building of theatres and galleries, the endowing of artists, individually and in groups, and assisting performing artists to tour. In other words, it has largely been in terms of masonry and money. We have yet to learn whether this activity has any effect on the creation of art, good or null. It will most likely have a favorable effect on interpretive art — the performance of music, of dance, of plays. As for the rest, we do not yet know, and the subject is clouded by imponderables that prohibit prophecy. If statistics are taken as chief guide, as they are in such a vulgar and distorted book as *The Culture Consumers* by Alvin Toffler, then the cultural explosion could turn out to be one of the worst disasters in the artistic life of this country: an approach that equates the clicking of museum turnstiles with the growth of taste. Just think of the millions who filed past Michelangelo's "Pietà" at the New York World's Fair. If they had been truly affected by it, they would have come out and burned down the rest of the Fair.

The chief safeguard against what we may call numerism is progressive, unpetrified elitism. Fine art is not for everybody, Tolstoy and his disciples notwithstanding. Democracy is a political theory, not an aesthetic one. Any teacher who is not an advocate of elitism, who does not approach the subject of art as the abbot of a religious order approaches novices to find out which ones truly have the vocation, instead of trying to recruit them all — such a teacher is in my view a menace.

A word must be said about the manifestations of art that preponderate. We are all well aware these days that in the world of art, fine art does not exist alone. It coexists with popular art, which in the last two hundred years or so has grown in proportionate amount and in influence. This growth has zoomed since the Second World War, for reasons that are familiar. Mass culture is now so large, so pervasive, that it cannot be omitted from any discussion of art. In the audience arts — films, the theatre, television — mass culture is so important and employs so many skilled people that it is rightfully in the province of serious criticism. No serious literary critic would concern himself with the latest best-selling historical romance simply because it was decently constructed and bearably written. But a serious film critic might well have to concern himself with the film made from that book because of the executant artists concerned, who may for various reasons have to operate within commercial films only and whose work needs comment, and because the power — in dream and fantasy — of the film version of the novel is so enormously intensified that it becomes both more influential and more interesting. Besides, fine art of our day often uses some of the modes and manners of the mass art. For example, in the theatre, *Guys and Dolls* raised musical comedy to a new dimension; in films *Dr. Strangelove* grew out of science fiction and popular topical fiction.

Two points can be concluded from this, I believe: (1) no firm line can be drawn between fine art and popular art; (2) equally, they are not mistakable one for the other. The moviegoer who doesn't like a good Western is malnourished and contemporaneously malformed; the polemicist of the popular who tells us that Westerns, or similar pictures, are what films are *for* is also malformed. There can no longer be any doubt that fine art derives some vitality, some ideas of method, some tonalities, from popular art, and by no means always in terms of parody or patronization or — if I may use an already tedious word — camp. Similarly, for the cultivated person, there is little doubt — in the vast majority of instances — as to what is fine art, even when it uses popular elements. One rough definition might be that fine art aims to be more than it seems, aims to have resonances larger than its materials. The popular has no such aim. It often does have such resonances, but they are incidental and accidental. Fine art is the use of experience as illumination; popular art is experience as entertainment. Popular art can take care of itself; the very essence of its being is that it thrives without subsidy, support, or study or else it dies. It is or is not. Fine art needs all those elements that popular art can scorn, plus some cultivation—some training—of its audience.

The surge and power of popular art, its constant and rightful appearance as a subject of serious discussion, have further muddled a clear view of artistic standards. The necessity to understand the relevance of popular art is sometimes misconstrued as an argument for alteration of standards. I think it is simply an argument for greater catholicity. It would be a failure in the teaching of art to ignore the existence and value of the popular. It would be a further facet of democratic sentimentality to equate it, in any degree, with serious art. And this is not to say that the standards of art are fixed. They are like the rules of grammar: if there are not rules, there is no grammar; but they must respond to life, usage, pertinence.

Let me now move on to the specific art in which that confusion is most likely to occur — the film — not to define further the differences between the popular and the fine, but to comment on some benefits of the latter. I scant the drama because, as far as the secondary school is concerned, the drama is treated much like literature, with the exception that it can be read aloud in class — assigning roles to different students — a device which, if it is not necessarily enlightening, is at least an antidote to possible boredom.

Film is quite a different matter. It has a number of assets, which I'll come to, and one fundamental advantage it shares with only one other art. It comes to the student exactly in the form in which it was made by the artist. This is true of only one other art — literature of the English language. Recorded music is wonderful, but it is not in the form intended by the composer. Reproductions of painting, photographs, models of architecture, and translations of foreign literature, all these are often excellent; none is the original work of art. Only literature in English and the film are available in a classroom exactly as they came from the maker's hand. They are thus the two arts that are safest from intrusions of middlemen enroute, including teachers, and since film has some unique powers and attractions, it is, in that sense, the safer of the two.

I must be clear that I'm speaking about films that have been made as art, not educational films, such as the Encyclopaedia Britannica films in the humanities or factual films meant to instruct. These are educational tools, which may or may not be good; they stand in relation to the films I'm discussing as textbooks and syllabus guides stand to literature. The films I mean are the ones available in the many catalogs of film rental firms, the ones that have been made and shown all over the world as works of some degree of art. They are available in 16-millimeter prints, and all you need in order to bring American or Swedish or Japanese or Indian artists making art into a classroom in Ashtabula or Tucson is a 16-millimeter projector and a modest budget.

I'll skip any exegesis of the general values of artistic experience for those capable of it and concentrate on some specific values of film:[1]

---

1. Some of the following material is adapted from the essay, "The Film Generation," in my book *A World on Film* (New York: Harper and Row, 1966).

1. In an age imbued with technological interests, this is the one art that flowers out of technology. Excepting architecture, film is the one art that can capitalize directly on the twentieth-century luxuriance of applied science. Some composers and some sculptors are trying to bridge the gap between art and science with the use of electric and electronic components. The film-maker has no choice; he *must* use electronic equipment. This contributes to a sense of junction with his society, with membership in the present. The technological interest and the interest in applied science of American youth are notable, not to say notorious. I think they and the audiences of all ages share the film-maker's feeling of union with the present, perhaps unconsciously; I think that the scientific skills involved are in themselves a link between them and the artist. Lately we have heard much of Marshall McLuhan's thesis that "the medium is the message." Insofar as McLuhan is not a salesman of McLuhan, there is some insight to be found in his work, and insofar as these insights have relevance to future society, they certify that this technological ambience of films is of prime socio-cultural importance.

2. Through the film, the world of surfaces and physical detail has again become material for art. Young people, if they are anything more than clods, are professional discoverers, and in no way are they more alert than to their physical environment. The film has taken over from the novel the primary function of creating material reality. It has exalted this function, for instead of merely making a mosaic of details into

which life also fits, the film manages to create poetry out of doorknobs, breakfasts, and furniture. Trivial details, of which everyone's universe is made, can once again be transmuted into metaphor, contributing to imaginative act.

A complementary, powerful fact is that this principle operates whether the film-maker is concerned with it or not. In any film except those with fantastic settings, whether the director's aim is naturalistic or romantic or symbolic or anything else, the physical world, through the mysteries of photography, never stops insisting on its presence and relevance.

This phenomenon gives some verity even to many mediocre films and gives great vitality to a film by a good artist. Indeed, out of this phenomenon, it can be argued that the film discovered pop art half a century ago, digested this minor achievement, then continued on its way.

3. The film form as such seems particularly apt for the treatment of many of the pressing questions of our day. I don't think this an inappropriate point in relation to high school students who, I am told, read Hemingway, Faulkner, and Pasternak. Nor do I mean by "pressing questions" such limited adolescent questions as juvenile delinquency. Such a film, for example, as *The Sound of Trumpets* by the young Italian, Ermanno Olmi, is one that any responsive high school student could appreciate and should see — a film about a youth's first job in an immense corporation in Milan.

The film form's particular strength in this area is its ability to externalize certain psychical matters that, for example, the theatre cannot easily deal with; it can relate them to physical environment in a manner that the theatre cannot contain nor the novel quite duplicate. The film can dramatize post-Freudian man, his habitat, and the relation between the two.

4. Film is, as I have noted, the one art that is available to the whole world at once, exactly as it was first made. With subtitles, it is the only art involving language that can be enjoyed in a language of which one is ignorant. (I except opera, where the language rarely needs to be understood precisely.)

The point is not the spreading of information or amity, as in USIA or UNESCO films; the point is emotional relationship and debt. If one has been moved by, say Japanese actors in Japanese settings, in actions of Japanese life that have resonated against one's own experience, there is a connection with Japan that is deeper than the benefits of propaganda or travelogue.

Obviously similar experience — emotional and spiritual — is available through other arts but rarely with the imperial ease of the film. As against foreign literature, foreign films have an advantage besides accessibility in the original language. The Japanese novelist invites us to re-create the scene in imagination. The Japanese film-maker provides the scene for us with a vividness that our minds cannot equal in a foreign setting. Thus our responses can begin at a more advanced point and can more easily, although not more strongly, be stimulated and heightened. This universality and this relative simultaneity of response have made us all members of a much larger empathetic community than has been immediately possible before in history.

5. Film has one great benefit by accident — its youth — which I believe makes it especially attractive to the young. The motion-picture camera is only about seventy-five years old, and that's a generous estimate. It is this freshness, relative to the other arts, that gives young people not only the excitement of the potentials of the form but a strong proprietary feeling about it. The film belongs to them.

These are five of the reasons why, I believe, films can be of special interest and effect with young people — why I believe they are important in any curriculum concerned with culture. I repeat an earlier reason — the film is the art form probably best insured against the teaching of culture, against the rough usage it must get at the hands of most teachers and the possible blunting to which it is liable even in the hands of good teachers in the routines of the classroom and the processes of explication.

But this statement needs counterbalance. Despite the statistics of the cultural explosion, we seem to be living in the end of an age of belief in the death of art. Ever since Flaubert, we have been hearing about the death of the novel; composers are telling us that both tonality and atonality are finished; painters are telling us that art as planned mimesis — even mimesis of the imagination or fantasy — is finished. Whether the term "finished" is accurate or not, certainly all the arts are going through profound metamorphoses. It is so clear that old forms within each art are dying, that belief in that truth is no longer a useful progressive tenet. We may find out before the end of this century whether a new culture is possible or whether all cultural life is going to divide into two phases — museum-keeping and mere activity — or whether there will be a third phase. Museum-keeping I define as the obvious with painting and sculpture but also as the maintenance of repertories of Shakespeare and Ibsen, of Beethoven and Bach, of libraries of Dickens and Yeats. Mere activity I define as, for example, most chance music, action or pop or op painting, underground cinema, Park Avenue architecture.

The third function — about which we cannot yet tell — is the possible evolution of a new pertinent culture, relevant to the new societies that are going to keep evolving one after another, possibly with increasing rapidity, a culture with a relationship analogous to that of previous cultures with previous societies, in terms of affirmation of community, a source of inspiration and consolation. There is no guarantee that art is not dying — all art; that it will not be completely supplanted by arty activity — for a while — until even that dies out. But neither is there a guarantee that art will die. A relevant and vital future culture may be possible if, in the process of metamorphosis, we adapt but do not jettison the standards that thousands of years of art have given us.

Among the strongest facts militating toward the survival of art — toward a new socially pertinent art that is sensibly derivative of the past — is the fact of the film. And this is where the schools come in: the creation of an audience that *demands* film that is true — that is socially and culturally apposite yet reflective of human history — is, as I said at the outset, one way to insure that we will *get* the film that we would like to have. One way to create that audience is for those young people who might constitute that audience to get early exposure to good films — maximum exposure with maximally helpful discourse.

In short, to put it in reverse order, the high school teachers of this country can expose their classes to good films; and the susceptible members of those classes may become the audience that can do much to evoke good films in the future. Those future good films may help to bridge the passage from a disintegrating cultural age to the integration of another without losing our rich heritage. It is a large statement and a large order; but then, why shouldn't it be?

ROBERT SHAW

The Conservative Arts

MY PARTICULAR ASSIGNMENT from Harold Taylor for
this symposium on humanism for young humans was
to "write on what you would like to see happen in the
high schools as far as music is concerned — not only
the playing, composing, singing, and all that, but the
effect of the musical arts on the high school environment." Knowing a bit of his turn of mind, I was not
inordinately surprised at his lack of concern that I
really had had very little sustained experience at encouraging young humans to be humanists — or joust-
ing with windmills for that matter.

I read a week ago Dr. Friedenberg's contribution to
this symposium, and I felt somehow comfortably sustained by his pessimism. To his — the social and educational organisms being what they are — "it can't be
done," I would have added "and besides, high
school is much too late." And, worse yet, perhaps for

our and the world's society "it's *all* too late."

It embarrasses me to remind myself that of all the people involved in this symposium, my experience with the arts and education probably is the most severely restricted. I have had rather intensive daily contact for a quarter of a century with a branch, generally regarded as minor, of a single art. Recent years have widened that experience to include other instruments and phenomena of the musical scene, and there have been a dozen or more summers substantially taken with the teaching materials and methods to choral conductors — many of them employed in the high school fields — but not until this past summer did I undertake a project of musical study and performance with high school students.

I strongly suspect, however, that a great deal of what I will end up saying will be not so much objective, statistical, and critical as it will be personal and moralistic.

Let me trace in a very few words the probable trajectory of my discourse: (1) the humanities — with the arts — offer the most hopeful handle to a sane, happy productive life and society; (2) an intense, active relationship to one or more of the creative (performing) arts is the surest approach to the attitudes and enlightenments of the humanities; and (3) if we were really to introduce such a program in our secondary schools, we would not only turn present curricula upside down and inside out, forcing changes in pre- and post-high school curricula, but we would further demand changes of our entire society, political, economic, and philosophical.

All of us here are committed to the humanities. We have a new set of foundation-subscribed investigations to prove a cultural explosion in urban America. We can point to direct federal aid to the arts and enormously expanding independent foundational subsidies. This is all faintly reassuring, even if one notes that a surprising amount of such funds find their way into building projects, and even if one notes the infinitesimal percentile the arts of concord receive versus the sciences of conflict — or the humanities versus the inhumanities.

Somehow before I can answer Dr. Taylor's question, I have to know for myself again *why* the arts are this important. For it seems to me that while we may modestly and properly estimate the immediate effects and influence of this small gathering, what we are actually proposing is that the values our schools and society and polity are run by are the wrong ones. We are proposing that the participative arts and the humanities are a better guide to productive and meaningful living than, at least, the statistical sciences and commercial trainings.

For some months now I have been fondling a phrase called "the conservative arts." Two summers ago I was one of the commencement speakers at the University of Alaska. These ceremonies were on a Monday afternoon, and I arrived in Fairbanks early enough to hear Sunday's baccalaureate address delivered by the chief chaplain of the U.S. Army, a full general as I recall. His advice to the graduating classes, in which there were a number of masters and doctorate degrees represented, was twofold. First, to the women he recommended that, now they had their education, it were best to forget it and settle down to the business of building a nest, pleasuring a man, and raising young, and the implication was not to be missed that an education for women, especially one concerned with the liberal arts, need not be an insurmountable obstacle to the real business of life if one had a good forgettery. Second, to the men of the classes he admonished that from the Alaskan mainland on a clear day you could see Communism forever and greater honor was available to no man than to lay down his life ag'in it, and apparently as frequently as possible.

I had but recently returned from a tour of Russia with a chorus and chamber orchestra as part of our cultural exchange program. For six weeks we had toured a somewhat narrow north-to-south corridor, giving thirty concerts in eleven cities. The program was almost exclusively religious music, because that is the historical nature of the choral repertoire and because the Soviet ministry of "atheistic" culture had requested Bach's *Mass in B Minor*.

The tour corresponded precisely with the sharp edge of the Cuban crisis, and where we might have expected to meet demonstrations or picketing, there were only affectionate greetings of "bravo" and "thank you." There were near riots preceding all *B Minor Mass* performances, due only to the throngs of people unable to gain entrance; and the night of its final performance it was broadcast in its entirety — including lengthy intermissions and ovations — throughout the entire Iron Curtain complex. For three hours the only fare available to this "materialistic, atheistic" audience was this monument of Christian creed, philosophy, and art – through their offices.

Gifts proffered in return for the pleasure they said they had received were abstract paintings in the manner of Mondrian and Pollock and, even more poignantly, contemporary ikons out of Mother Russia by Grecoesque twentieth-century distortionists. (What a strange twist to find the avant-garde, the independent, and rebellious young linked to religious expression. In my college days it was considered hopelessly vulgar to be any less than agnostic.)

Here is a fraction of a translation of a review published in the *Russian State Journal of Arts* following our return to the United States:

> In what lies the immortality and eternal beauty of Bach's music? Why does it so excite, please, and move people at all times, including us, the people of the middle twentieth century? Probably every generation has given and gives its own answer to these questions.
>
> The spiritual life of modern man is infinitely complicated. His thinking, memory, and aesthetic feeling are constantly developing, but still the human principles that are characteristic of man were and remain immutable. They rest on principles simple and eternal as the world itself: humanism, truth, good, beauty.
>
> All this the music of Bach reveals to us in forms which are simple and majestic, clear, and infi-

nitely wise. The music sings of life. It uplifts us, forces us not only to rejoice and to suffer but, most of all, to think.

My point is certainly not that the political and economic problems of the world are going to be solved by going singing together. Economic and political problems exist, and they have to be solved economically and politically. But I drew two conclusions from that experience, reinforced by similar tours of twenty-one countries in the Middle East and Europe, and nine in South America. A generous and lively exchange in the liberal and performing arts can accomplish some things: it can gain us time, and it can give us the hope that if we understand each other so warmly and naturally in these areas, we may one day be able to compose political and economic differences.

One other thing occurred to me on the plane flying back. In general the intellectual and moral climate of our times is agreeable to the proposition that man does not live by bread alone. (In Westchester County and other suburbia they have it that man does not live by grass alone.) And it is precisely this interchange in the humanities — medicine, architecture, poetry, philosophy, and music among them — that *is* and *should be* the business of man. This is the dream that this justifies political and economic activity and validates it. Man does not live by bread, grass, economics, or politics alone. These adventures in exchange at the highest level of human aspiration shine as a sort of beacon — that it has happened, that it can happen, and that it *must* happen here and now.

All this and a good deal more became my angry answer on the morrow in Alaska to the chaplain leader's address. Mine was titled "The Conservative Arts," and I found a delight in the adjective, such as Charles Addams might find in Mother's Day — "Say it with fungus." For, of course, what I had very earnestly in mind was the *liberal* arts — so called, tradition says, because their study in Roman days was accorded only to free men — and, even of these liberal arts, that portion of them which we designate as "creative" or "performing" or occasionally "seven and lively," or nowadays, and a little more broadly, the "humanities."

Reluctantly I had to conclude to myself that "conservative" was not a dirty word. In spite of the contemporary cross- and backfire of piosity and poison, Judased and prejudiced from either side, impregnable no less than ill-conceived, if conservative can mean literally "conserving, preserving," then the title has made its point. What do the liberal creative arts conserve? Perhaps nothing — but humanity. The argument, then, behind the title is that the arts, and probably in direct ratio as to how liberal, creative, and active they are, are the preservers and purveyors of those values which define humanity (and for some define Divinity) and finally, in fact, may prove to be the only workable program of conservation for the human race on this planet.

I hope you will forgive me if I now restate some of my thinking on that occasion in Alaska. It cannot be new to any of you, but it forms the mulch out of which my attempts to answer Dr. Taylor's question must grow. I asked myself a series of questions:

What are the meanings of art? What is it trying to tell us of man? What is man trying to tell us of himself?

Second, what may be the function or influence of art in a world gone schizophrenic, pustulant, and masochistic?

What occurred to me immediately was that if we could consider for a moment that Russians and Cubans and even south by southeast Americans were also human, then the answers to the first question might also tell something concerning question number two. And it occurred to me further that if we were to inquire into the nature of art, we might very well end by pondering the nature of man — a study proper enough.

We face two facts of this here-now life: (1) man teeters on the brink of self-annihilation, and (2) quoting the butcher, baker, candlestick maker, "I don't see what I possibly can do to stop it."

Fact of life number one — governments, not for any lack of earnestness or endeavor, possibly even without malice, and for reasons which must be disturbingly unknown, even to themselves, engage hourly and horrifyingly in a juggling and counter-juggling of propagandas, munitions, monies, and men uncertifiable even by the laws of average. And, I asked myself parenthetically, "Is man really worth saving?" Certainly all those born last night are. And an eight-year-old son is and everybody's children in college — none of whom has had the opportunity to merit the wind he inherits — are. But, in spite of Socrates, Jesus, Beethoven, Shakespeare, Lincoln, Buddha, Gandhi, and a host of lesser saints, is it not possible to paraphrase the psalmist, "When I consider this earth, the work of my fingers, the *horrors* I have created, what is man that he is mindful of himself?"

Might it just be that man is *not* worth saving?

There came immediately another question, and it was really a half-answer. On the other hand — "Could it be possible that human life itself — unclassified — is a plus on creation's side?" Not, is *this* life or *that* life worth saving? Not even, is it worth killing for? But, in view of the timeless, consciousless upward climb of warm mud to cold man, is the life-force in the man-thing of itself a value, and enough to save him from self-destruction?

When the table stakes are raised from trade routes and development rights, through principalities and powers to man himself — absolute or obsolete — the game is not the same.

Fact of life number two — the lonely sickness in each man's soul — familiar no doubt as well to kings, prime ministers, and presidents as to students, teachers, musicians, and bartenders — that there is, indeed, very little that "I can do about it." This provoked me to write:

> They say this world
> Is smaller now.
> —But not my world.
> My world is full
> Of hurricane and tide,
> Of flux and flood,
> Of thrusts and space
> I never thought to face.
> And still no place
> To hide.

The jailer of Paul and Silas at Philippi, originator of "What must I do to be saved?" was panicked only by an earthquake at midnight, not by "How will you have your cities this morning, with or without people?" or "How do you like your children, crisp or scrambled?"

Which of us, simply by accident of being born and in personal as well as public affairs, does not find himself on a runaway rocket blasting a trackless blackness, speed and destination out of sight, mind, and control? "What is man? And, can he be saved?"

It was my conviction then, as now, that an attention to the conservative liberal arts might give us more than half-answers and some hope.

I did not list or define these arts, first, because there is little uncertainty as to where in general they lie — certainly among the humanities — and second, because I held a suspicion that in the end art may prove to be as much an attitude as an aptitude and more a point of view than a product. When I say "art," then, know that I mean now the languages and produce of Beethoven, Shakespeare, Donatello, Bach, Dickinson, El Greco, Picasso, Melville, and a host of others.

What does this sort of art show itself to be, why is it important, and how can it help us? I found for myself four answers:

1. Art on this scale is the most pervasive, persistent, powerful affirmation of the life-force in the man-thing. Than Sex it is stronger and longer — by centuries and oceans. It is regeneration, reincarnation, and the "agony of resurrection." It is a true transubstantiation — pitch into sonata, form into spirit, paint onto canvas

into tears, words onto paper across a proscenium into the heart of man — Essence inferred into substance achieved, in order to communicate Essence. Ally through all time of the evolutionary thrust, it is finally the Flesh become Word.

2. In the face of Chaos, art is the recognition of isolate identity and the achievement of Order. Facing the myriad phenomena of sensation, it is the ability to isolate the singular and the significant — that edge of color, this moment of pitch, yea, this chip of marble — and so place it in the company of other identities, equally select and positioned so that the solo of the Whole is greater than the Chorus of its parts.

> Out of Chaos
> A spirit moving over
>   the face of the waters
> Out of the random a rule,
> Out of the countless and contrary
> The mark of One.

For Pattern and Order are very precious to Art, and they form the center of its meaning.

> Matters of proportion —
>   the relations of tone, timbre, and texture
>   line rhythm and tempo
>   expectation, continuation
>   recurrence, closure —
> are not grandmother's eboned and
>   polished clothing tree
>   dunce-capped and slack-coated
>   while love is made in the parlour.

They are root, trunk, branch, and leaf —
  seed, sap, and substance of Art's meaning
Art is the achievement of Order.

3. The third aspect of art's meaning I found elo-
quently stated in a book of an English mathematician,
J. W. N. Sullivan, entitled *Beethoven, His Spiritual
Development*. It was Mr. Sullivan's contention that
during the past few decades the mechanistic theories
which ruled man's thinking for some three hundred
years have been severely shaken. Science has been able
to provide knowledge of matter but not of essence.
Therefore, matters of value, which heretofore have
been ignored because they were not measurable, may
still have something to say concerning the nature of
reality.

A work of art may indeed be a "revelation." The
"higher consciousness" of the creative artist is evi-
denced not only by his capacity of ordering his
experience but also by the capacity of having his
experience.

The reason that our reaction to a work of art cannot be adequately described is not that some
unique and isolated faculty is involved but that
art is not superfluous, that it exists to convey
that which cannot be otherwise conveyed.

There is, after all, in man's being a mystery, and it is
peculiarly the discretion of great art not to elucidate
but to illumine the unknown — without engraving its
image.

4. The fourth mark of art's meaning I find in the simple fact that it is unremittingly an attempt to communicate, to establish contact, to find kinship even across centuries and oceans. It does seem to me that political and economic configurations — and their facets running hot and cold — are more frequently divisive than comprehensive.

It is to the credit of art and the arts that, except for short periods when they have been subverted by politics or principles not their own — as in Hitler's Germany or Stalin's Russia — they have been a unifying force in the affairs of men, have promoted understanding and affection rather than half-truth and no-trust. Art has instituted no crusades, has burned neither witches nor books. Indeed, in this respect, and parhaps because it has not been so institutionalized, great art, even more than established religion, has been the open hand of man reaching for another's and the persistent focus of his good will.

These maybe at least are some of the meanings of art — and advertently of mankind.

Where I find myself as I face Harold Taylor's specific assignment is on a spot very like this:

I believe that those areas of human concern, conjecture, and commitment which we call the humanities have more to tell us of the nature of man and the organization of his social environment than areas of information isolated by design or chance from those humanities.

I believe that the humanities are best approached not by passive examination, analysis, and historical survey, but by active participation in one or more of the creative arts.

And I believe that where such involvement in the creative arts occurs, at a very early stage self-expression and enjoyment, if they do not do so of themselves, must be guided to intersect with disciplines of technique, form, style, and history. This ought to occur naturally and enthusiastically but must never be by-passed.

And, as it seems to me all this presumes an eruptive violent reorientation, not only of educational organisms but also of a great part of our society, it is difficult to be practical and at the same time optimistic.

Certainly, for instance, high school is too late. It is not necessarily too late for the single student, but it is late for the family of man. (For me, for instance, early grade school art is characterized by high individuality and humor, while high school painting already begins to betray its conformities.) Still, there has to be some hope until confirmed adulthood — and perhaps we can work backwards from high school.

A high school music program has to begin with standards of *literature* and *performance*, and in neither regard is compromise tolerable. The young person of high school age has the intelligence, vitality, and physical ability to cope with a considerable amount of the world's great music, and to give him anything other than this or to demand less than a near-professional standard of performance is to betray both the student and the art.

The original sin in music education is the choice or toleration of mediocre materials. The Friday, Saturday, and Sunday afternoon football band extravaganzas cost annually certainly no less than millions of student hours of marching, arching, practicing, prancing, preening, and undoubtedly hundreds of thousands of friends' and parents' dollars for the latest in costumery; and it has to be 99 44/100 per cent pure and missionary mediocrity. I started to say "unabashed," but it occurs to me that so infrequently does this experience lead to mature musical enjoyment and participation that there must be considerable postgame embarrassment.

People know now that there are standards in musical literature. They know that there is good music and bad music. This is true not only technically but in terms of aesthetics and taste and, if we can accept Sullivan's hypothesis, additional areas of meaning, some of them very close to the ethical and moral.

People also know that good music exists in varying degrees of technical difficulty. It is not impossible to supply the earnest beginner with something *worth* playing or singing. With the appearance of the weak piece, a sense of embarrassment settles over the earnest amateur chorus. The contemporary plague of Malotte's *The Lord's Prayer* cannot for long convince anyone who has to perform it, simply because it has a wow of a lyric.

It is supportable now that so-called "great music" is great not because it has been so decreed in New York, London, Vienna, or Moscow, by the contemporary society of sophisticates, but because it continues to say something so universal and so essential and native to even the humblest of involved seekers that not even performing it well will diminish its miracle. I have further had enough experience in performing undoubted but presumed evasive and recondite masterworks before presumed frontier audiences to know that the most earnest and best made music reaches most generally and deeply the person who takes pride in his own craft, however removed from the arts it may appear.

Only the finest music ultimately can involve, energize, and seed the human thing, can help make a whole man out of a half-child. In high school we are offering a diet of well over eighty-five per cent commercially reconstituted bushwah.

In two other areas we have largely fumbled our repertoire responsibilities. The first regards the authoritative professional produce of our own time. It came as a great surprise to the entire musical world that Tom Hilbish could train a Princeton high school chorus to professionally definitive performances of a Webern cantata. The facts are that by his own enthusiasm and know-how he enabled these young people to make contact with the important sounds of their own time. Guided by him the works of their near-contemporaries became their teachers. The musical contributions of their day became a language they could hear, read, and recite.

We cannot afford to ignore, particularly with young people, even that portion of today's musical produce which may seem to us utter nonsense. We witness today the avoidance of musical systems and order, deferring to an aural construction submissive to calculated disorder or disorder-by-chance, or we listen to aural orders constructed without reference to human or humanly produced sounds. This latter invites a consideration of the social aspects of musical performance, for traditionally it has been a participative art. Music has been the product of a simultaneous common endeavor. In this it has been unlike the visual arts and the literary arts, with the exception of drama, with their one-to-one ratio of creator to consumer. The tape composer certainly has within the powers of his medium the apparent opportunity of establishing a relationship with his consumer parallel, if not in all respects similar, to that of the poet and the painter.

The areas of chance, silence (nonmusic), electronic and taped configurations, have in our time to be explored and experienced by our young people. Reading about them in *Newsweek* will not "humanize."

In another area we are all but one hundred per cent remiss. Somewhere along the line provision has to be made for training in composition at the high school level and for performances by student forces. This is not at all an impractical idea. Part-time specialists are available in most urban areas. And this is the entire and inevitable cap of creative involvement.

I have one other thing to say about repertoire, and that is that it ought to be selected as offering the possibility of *complete* performance. That is to say, the presentation in performance of excised and mutilated works or of works for which some elements of the composer's musical forces are not available is of dangerously fragmented value. In a conscientious and comprehensive musical program these obstacles can frequently be overcome by merging forces with other community groups, adult or adolescent, amateur or professional. In the main, a composer's musical meaning is not to be separated from the sounds he heard in his inner ear and the instrumental and vocal forces he prescribed as to character and number.

This returns me for a moment to my initial position concerning music in the high school, namely that it has to begin with *repertoire* and *performance,* and that compromise in the standards of neither is acceptable. We have discussed a few of the aspects of repertoire. With reference to performance I had two things in mind. The first was that I can't see any value to a study of music which is entirely passive and reflective. To put it bluntly, music is not a consumers' art, and any approach to music which does not actively involve a person in playing or singing with, or composing for, some other person or persons is just so much nonsense.

A *participating listening* can indeed be taught. Ear training and dictation are a necessary part of every musician's technique. But this is a rigorous and extremely active discipline. And to assume that an appreciation of music can be taught via phonograph excerpts and predigested biographical vignettes is to accept the standard of the lay-back listener who proclaims, "I may be tone-deaf, but I know what I like."

My second point in regard to performance and compromise is that if materials are chosen intelligently and students are trained adequately, no compromise is necessary. I value, of course, the necessity and the gain of studying music which at a given time, for a variety of good reasons, may be impossible to perform. But this is a private study and practice under an awareness of present limitations. But those things which are presented publicly to others are not to be so selected and similarly used.

So far as I can tell, the young person of late high school age is very near his optimum physical and mental energies. Certainly in time he will add substantially to his knowledge and experience, which may add to his wisdom, but in terms of sheer vitality, agility, and, I think, a moral sensibility which may be a product of his first cognizance of compromise in the home and world about him, he's a very likely prospect to understand and demand of himself the highest standards of performance.

The most convincing thing in music is that magical fraction of an instant when everything is actually in tune, or when a real undisguisable ensemble eighth-note follows a dotted quarter. Once a chorus or orchestra has experienced these and one or two other comparable precisions, it never can be the same. Rightness convinces not because it is commanded but because it is in the nature of the material. In experiencing the joys of the knowledge of a composer's meaning no amount of goodwill can substitute for right notes.

A mastery and understanding of the arts is only to be gained through a self-tyranny of concentration. There is no escaping physical, mental, and emotional exhaustion. High school's a good age to carry it.

Now, what about the organization of a musical program so motivated? What sort of groups and studies would it entail?

Our premise will be that emphasis must be moved from those musical activities and organizations whose nature is largely social or whose function is not primarily musical to those groups where the art and the craft are first and where individual responsibility has a chance to grow. Insofar as instrumental groups are concerned, we certainly must face and conquer the all-consuming ogre of the pep- and marching-band. A concert band has some reason for existence in its repertoire and its educational possibilities, but there is a much grander, more varied, and more instructive repertoire for woodwind quintets, brass ensembles, and sonatas with piano accompaniment. Jazz ensembles have a real and valuable place here.

The orchestra is, of course, the richest of ensemble instrumental literature and should be the center of an instrumental program. This presupposes an active string program in the grade schools and junior high schools. Here again, the *main development* in the orchestral program should be the formation and instruction of chamber music ensembles — string quartets, piano trios, and the like, all manner of small ensembles which demand and encourage individual responsibility and creativity.

Insofar as vocal groups and instruction are concerned, the mixed chorus of eighty to one hundred voices is a viable instrument for most works with orchestral accompaniment, except those which probably ought not yet to be attempted with altogether young voices. A chamber chorus of thirty or forty voices opens up another vastly exciting contemporary and preclassical repertoire, and madrigal groups of five to eleven or twelve voices have a repertoire all but limitless. The smaller instrumental and vocal ensembles have an extraordinary combined repertoire in the Renaissance, Baroque, and recent contemporary periods. That such direction and ensemble experience must be adequately supported by reasonably frequent drills in the rudiments of musicianship and by instruction, both class and private, in vocal and instrumental techniques will be apparent to all.

There are two additional areas I would heartily recommend for development in a high school music curriculum. In each of these, isolated and short-term programs have been initiated and experience gained, but their existence is insufficient and infrequent.

The first is a program of introducing into daily school life a sequence of musical professionals: a composer in residence (a handsome production project of the Ford Foundation administered by the National Musical Council and Music Educators National Conference) who writes music for the local forces and who certainly could counsel any gifted youngster; resident, or at least temporarily resident, chamber music groups — string quartets, woodwind quintets, and the like — to play for general student-body enjoyment and to coach their respective repertoire and instruments; and the use of local musically qualified professionals to do part-time teaching on the instruments and in the studies of their training and experience. This could conceivably effect a balance with those incomparably "accredited" teachers who have accumulated all manner of information except a knowledge of their subject.

In one other respect I should like to see, from place to place, a local investigation and development. It seems strange to me to isolate a high school education from the world outside its walls. I think this is important in music. High school students belong to the human race and to the adult human race. It seems to me that every city large enough to have a high school or two should be able to devise some productive musical activity or activities in which younger and older adults could mingle, study, and make music together. There are a score of ways such a project could be effected, most of them determined by local considerations.

We have not investigated modern teaching aids, for instance, those allied with teaching language, which surely must have some pertinence to the teaching of music. Certainly these will come in time. In addition we have said nothing about other and concurrent art programs — cinematography, dance, drama, painting, sculpture, and poetry, for example. It is humanly impossible for these programs to go on in isolation from one another. It is inconceivable that they should not abound in companion projects and create their own programs of reciprocal entertainment and demonstration.

I must say that nothing appears to me very original in these suggestions, or personal, other than the agony and ecstasy of their critical timeliness — if it is not already too late. But they do seem to me, in general, a way to reach a rounded and responsible humanity. It is inconceivable to me, for instance, that one can learn music without learning something about dance. I have seldom, if ever, performed a piece of music with a symphonic chorus that at some final point in rehearsal did not dance, march, or otherwise improvise some physical movement throughout the entire two-and-one-half-hour rehearsal. I can't get rhythm or tone any other way. Similarly, it is unthinkable that a vocal work could be performed without the stuents' extensive investigation into its text sources, language structures, religious or national mythologies, and poetic sensibilities. Nor can I imagine a choir able to sing in tune which has not learned something about the nature of acoustics.

The hopeful affirmation is that the further we involve ourselves in one of the creative arts, the more nearly we touch the others, and the more meaningful and necessary become the systems of knowledge originally considered nonart.

What has to be said again is that this sort of thinking screams for an entirely new structure of educational organisms. In terms of time alone no less than half — and probably two thirds — of the student's time is proposed to be directed toward the humanities. Who, then, is to guide, and how is the remaining necessary or desirable knowledge to be organized? Does this thinking not lead us very nearly to a one-to-one ratio of teaching force to student force? What are the economics of such education? Where do these ideal young find what sort of place in adult society and economy?

Somebody is going to say that the humanities are not so much a series of related fields of knowledge but a way of considering the various importances of men and matter. An active involvement with one of the arts, even as late as high school, is a necessary step toward that attitude, and — even if it's too late — it's a chance.

EDGAR Z. FRIEDENBERG

A Teaching Credential for Philoctetes?

SINCE I AM THE MEMBER of this symposium whose work is least connected with the arts as such, I shall assume that my most useful function will be to discuss how the schools — whose mode of operation is my special professional interest — are involved in humanistic education, and how their limitations as social organisms set limits to what one may hope to undertake within them. I am not very hopeful that I shall come up with much in the way of practical suggestions. Discussions of curriculum have come to seem to me luxurious in much the same way that discussions of doctrinal variation within an established church seem to me luxurious. They may deal with very important issues, certainly, but the fact that time and energy are massively diverted into such refinements is in itself usually evidence that the church, as a social institution, is already pretty confident that it controls the lines of communication between man and God, however it may decide to organize them. What it decides to do is then usually less important than what it is and how it works. One need not know a word of Latin to be able to infer from Cardinal Cushing's tone of voice, as he intoned President Kennedy's requiem, that no modern equivalent of Chartres could be constructed in urban New England.

I shall direct my attention, then, not to the objectives of education in the humanities as curriculum specialists have stated and departments of education have adopted them nor to a survey of interesting new experiments in education in literature or the arts. Instead, I shall discuss how the school and its personnel affect the way in which humanistic experience may be created, transmitted, or aborted and how the function of the school as a social institution determines, distorts, or limits the kind of artistic experience with which the school may deal and the ways in which it may, and may not, deal with it. If I wished to put the matter more positively, I could speak instead of the role of the school in transmitting our artistic heritage and in furnishing an atelier and an audience for the creative work of adolescent artists. The topic would be the same; just as one may speak in a high school history course of the role of the monasteries in preserving the works of antiquity or, at a higher critical level, grieve that only those relics the Church could tolerate and monks could accept and appreciate were preserved.

Much of what American public schools do about artistic experience may be attributed to three of the schools' most basic social functions. They are familiar: the transmission of culture, the promotion of social mobility, and the assimilation of youth of diverse backgrounds into a common American culture. These functions of the school have complemented each other in contributing to our historical development; but the effect they have jointly produced is antagonistic to, and probably cannot encompass, humanistic education.

In order to transmit culture and promote social mobility simultaneously, the schools have had to accept and act upon the commonplace assumption that artistic experience is embodied in a set of objects whose value is attested by the regard in which successive generations of higher status individuals have held them. If one of the most important things education is supposed to do is teach youngsters how to operate successfully at a higher social level than their family enjoyed, then the schools must suppose themselves the custodians of artistic taste and must suppose that such taste is something that can be *conveyed* to persons who do not *possess* it — one learns to enjoy music or painting or wine as one might buy a car, not as one might rear a child and grow oneself in the process. In its crudest form, to be sure, this approach to art is outdated even in the schools and in popular culture: The concept of an art *object,* like that of a museum or a zoo in which magnificent but exotic treasures are isolated, is a nineteenth-, not twentieth-century idea. This is still the age of the culture-consumer, but the act of consumption is now supposed to be intimate and casual; the collector has been replaced by the participant.

But this seems to me to make very little fundamental difference in the relationship of the pupil to artistic experience. It is true that what is taught is now less often a naive catalog of classic works; instruction more often centers on the structure and dynamics by which the artist develops and exploits the possibilities of his medium, so that students come to understand some of the problems of expression in that medium and develop a basis for critical judgment. This is all to the good, but it does not alter the student's situation as much as it seems to. Instead of becoming a collector of objects or of reproductions of objects, he now becomes a collector of postures or of reproductions of postures. Where forty years ago a student might have been taught in art appreciation class that Cézanne and Ravel were modern classics, he would be taught today that to care whether they were or not was a sign of philistinism. Upper-middle-class people are now expected to involve themselves with the work rather than to prize it as the autograph of a star. But involvement, authenticity, and passion are now the conventional insignia of the educated individual's approach to the arts and, as such, are frequently forged by students who wish to convince themselves or others that they are participating in a creative experience. This has become the appropriate, institutionally patterned way for a latter-day bourgeois to respond to the arts; and the schools teach it as part of the pattern of middle-class life.

Leading students into this pattern of life and confirming them in a middle-class conception of themselves are the central functions of the public school system. But this means that the schools are designed to teach their pupils to behave in ways that anticipate the lives they hope to lead rather than to explore their life-in-progress. To the degree that schools take the humanities seriously, they violate their preparatory function; for the arts are meaningful only as they comment on life as the artist actually knows it, and the comment is intelligible only to persons who have in some degree shared the experience and the social context of the artist. I certainly do not disparage the value of artistic expression in equipping any of us to deal manfully with whatever the future may bring; on the contrary, the arts constitute our archive and our arsenal. They are the source both of the procedures and the materials that we use to bind our personal experience into a meaningful and durable basis on which to act, so that our life retains some consistent patterns as we live it. But precisely for that reason they are vitiated by instruction that teaches the student to look to the future rather than the present, and that breaks off pieces of the humanities to use as decorations or badges of membership.

Humanistic education, to be sure, transmits culture, and transmutes it as well, but not in a way that is useful to youngsters who seek to anticipate their experience rather than to examine it. It is just impossible either to create or understand the arts on credit. But humanistic education conflicts even more deeply with the schools' undertaking to promote the assimilation of youth from diverse ethnic or socio-economic backgrounds into the common WASPish pattern of American life. This may seem a strange contention; for the humanities are expected, above all, to promote mutual understanding among peoples. As Iago might have remarked to the Venetian Senate, had he been more liberal and optimistic: *Tout comprendre, c'est tout pardonner.*

But the crucial word is *tout*. Mutual understanding promotes acceptance among divergent people and groups only if it probes deeply enough to reach the common humanity that underlies their diversity. If it does not reach that deep, or if it does so only in spots, increased understanding is likely to exacerbate antagonism rather than to reduce it. In a democracy that holds to the image of a melting pot, public education serves to forestall excessive clarity of vision rather than to promote it. The schools, engaged as they are in mass education, have neither the resources nor the inclination to examine any highly significant work thoroughly enough to be certain that its integrative power will be stronger than its disruptive force. When the curriculum committee considers including *The Assistant* on the reading list for English, the one thing it can be sure of is that the Irish, the Jews, and the Flatbush Merchant's Association will all be insulted. Whether they will learn anything from it is more problematical.

Consequently, in their handling of the humanities, the schools do not so much fall into sentimentality as rely on it gratefully to deliver them from faction. Public education cements our society together by propagating an interlocking set of cliches that are not so much intended to convince as to disarm. Genuine artistic experience would remind students that, indeed, they already knew these cliches to be false, that our society consists of elements with strongly and basically con-flicting interests, that a tragedy is not just an unsolved problem nor sex a warm puppy, and that Gregor Samsa is one of the Beatles. Where would the Senior Honor Society hold its Citizenship Awards, if the auditorium were hung with Francis Bacon's paintings?

In order to socialize the young, which is what we hire them to do, the schools must systematically subvert the humanities. They must not only misrepresent and sentimentalize the meaning of reality, which is just what every artist must guard against as best he can, they must more subtly misrepresent the function of the arts themselves so that the revelatory edge is dulled and students do not learn to turn to them for liberation. This is not the accidental consequence of inadequate facilities or incompetent instruction; even when facili-ties are lavish and instruction sensitive and skilled — and in the modern high school they often are — some protection against the erosive effect of the arts on so-ciety must be built into the system. This is especially true in the secondary school, for it is in adolescence that our need for fidelity is strongest; one is more likely to demand that the artist "tell it like it is" then than at any other time, though only the most autonomous youths ever quite get to this point. That most do not, and remain fairly content to fulfill the routines that exist without asking themselves what is really happen-ing in their world or even how they could go about finding out, is education's major triumph. Our schools have become expert at driving cadmium rods into the seething mass of our cultural heritage and rendering it inactive. After Mr. Kennedy's assassination, high school students went right on reading *Macbeth* as if nothing had happened.

How is this done? Frequently by direct censorship: The school play is canceled, the student magazine is forbidden to publish a poem the adviser believes to be in questionable taste, or a teacher is fired for including in his syllabus a reading not on the state-approved list. It is important that anyone seriously engaged in considering the humanities curriculum remind himself that such events are commonplace in the public schools and are by and large accepted without significant protest by the communities the schools serve; they occur, indeed, only because the administration believes that more serious protest would arise if they did not. This recollection helps curriculum planners to stay realistic about the values and institutional climate of the social system they propose to modify. But except as testimony to how things are, direct censorship is a minor factor in debilitating the humanities curriculum. Much more serious obstacles to communication than overt censorship have been institutionalized in the very structure of the school system itself, and unless these structural characteristics are changed, they will block the effectiveness of any improvements that are made in the curriculum.

Among the most important of these is what teachers tend to be like. This, too, is changing; and my subjective but strong impression is that the quality of the high school teaching cadre is improving markedly, unless I am misleading myself by comparing the California teachers with whom I have recently been working with the urban Eastern teachers I had known earlier —

though there were good ones among these, too. In any case, I have had to revise my earlier picture to include a large proportion of teachers — mostly, I fear, assigned to schools in the more affluent districts — who handle literature, at least, with insight, competence, imagination, and respect for their learners. Nevertheless, one must recognize that the findings Guba, Jackson, and Bidwell[1] published several years ago are still more widely applicable than my most recent impressions as well as consistent with my earlier ones.

Using a paired-comparison type of questionnaire (the Edwards Personal Preference Schedule, which is derived from the yields results expressed in the same terms as the late Henry Murray's more familiar Thematic Apperception Test), with a sample of "366 public school teachers drawn from 24 schools in a nine-county area surrounding Chicago," Guba, Bidwell, and Jackson found:

> that the needs most characteristic of this group of teachers were high deference, order, and endurance and low heterosexuality, dominance, and exhibition . . . . The six needs may probably be taken as representative of an emergent occupational pattern found most prominently among what will be termed the "veteran teachers," that is, teachers of ten or more years' experience. Conspicuous by their absence are such needs as achievement, intraception, and nurturance, which

1. Egon G. Guba, Philip W. Jackson, and Charles E. Bidwell, "Occupational Choice and the Teaching Career," *Educational Research Bulletin,* vol. 38, 1959, pp. 1-12, 27.

might have been expected for a teacher group. Interestingly, the characteristics seem to fit the cultural stereotype of the teacher as sexually impotent, obsequious, eternally patient, painstakingly demanding, and socially inept. Again, it must be emphasized that these needs showed great variability, especially in regard to sex groups and length of teaching experience, and that therefore such sweeping generalizations will obviously be in error in a great many individual cases.

So they will and, I suspect, in an increasing proportion of individual cases as society, along with its corps of teachers, becomes less puritanical altogether. What Guba, Bidwell, and Jackson found seems to be essentially that teachers display the ideal typical characteristics of lower-middle-class *nebichness,* and the lower middle class is not quite as *nebich* as it used to be. Even in the period of less than a decade since their observations were made, teachers' salaries and their level of education have risen markedly, but their social status has not risen as much. Corwin[2] in his excellent new text observes:

> The conclusion is that while the standards of teaching have risen, as have teachers' salaries and their prestige relative to their past station, they have not risen greatly beyond the advances made by the general population, either in terms of general level of education, or the prestige of the vocational salaries of professional groups.

2. Ronald G. Corwin, *A Sociology of Education* (New York: Appleton-Century-Crofts, 1965), p. 228.

While something has gone wrong with the last phrase of that sentence, its implication is still clear enough. There is not much evidence to suggest that teaching is attracting, or is likely to attract, very different kinds of people from those it attracted when the Guba study was made; while its sample size was not large, the fact that its findings confirmed an established stereotype of what teachers are like does make its findings plausible. So far as humanistic education is concerned, the most important of the needs Guba, Bidwell, and Jackson found to characterize their group of teachers is the need to avoid *intraception.* By intraception Murray meant a need to look inward at the meaning of one's life and experience, to understand oneself and others subjectively, in contrast to the need, more fully developed in our culture, to observe external events and characteristics. Intraception is the very stuff of art, and it is significant, though not astonishing, that teachers should find it alien. Part of their job is to alienate young Americans from it.

But have we any evidence that what teachers are like, however unpromising they may appear from the viewpoint of the creative artist, does in fact have a repressive impact on their students? Unfortunately, yes, from a number of sources. The most explicitly relevant of these is Jacob W. Getzels and Phillip W. Jackson's remarkable study, *Creativity and Intelligence.*[3] Since I have had to make frequent use of this book in the years since its publication, I shall save myself a little time and effort by quoting from an extensive

---

3. (New York: Wiley, 1962).

summary I wrote about it on an earlier occasion in a professional publication:[4]

"Professors Jacob W. Getzels and Philip W. Jackson in their recent work on *Creativity and Intelligence* illustrate this process statistically. They drew their sample from a private, university affiliated high school which afforded them, I should judge, an unusually abundant supply of the kind of 'far-out' youngster that their methodology defines as creative. Their independent variables — that is, the criteria by which they assigned individual youngsters to their 'high-creative' group — are essentially measures of 'divergent thinking,' as Professor J. P. Guilford of the University of Southern California defines this kind of mental activity in contrast to the 'convergent thinking' of conventional high IQ students. Getzels and Jackson, in other words, started out by setting up a procedure in which the kind of adolescent who is especially prone to find a wealth of unconventional meanings in familiar material, and to use these meanings to arrive at perfectly workable but sometimes shockingly original solutions to the problems, was contrasted with the kind of adolescent who is adept at setting such meanings aside as distractions and marching with power and determination along the path of conventional wisdom.

"From a sample of 449 private high school students with a mean IQ of 129, Getzels and Jackson selected 26 students who were in the top 20 per cent on their Guilford-type measures of creativity, but not in IQ; and

4. "The School as a Social Environment," *The Behavioral Sciences and Education* (College Admissions 10) (New York: College Entrance Examination Board, 1963), p. 22-25.

28 who were in the top 20 per cent in IQ, but not in creativity. The two groups were then compared with each other and with the total group of 449 on school performance as measured by standard achievement tests; teachers' preferences for having them, when identified by name, in class; and the quality and manner of their response to a series of pictures like those used in the Thematic Apperception Test.

"Both groups did equally well on the subject-matter tests of school achievement, and better than the total group of 449. The teachers, however, preferred the high IQ students to both the high creatives and those who had not been included in either group; and though they did prefer the high creatives to the average student, the difference was too small to be statistically significant. It should be borne in mind that this was a private secondary school with an exceptionally intelligent student body, and teachers who, to some extent, had chosen to teach gifted students and were accustomed to them. But they nevertheless preferred school achievement to be expressed in conventional terms, which creatives were unlikely to do.

"Getzels and Jackson quote illustratively the following sample responses to one of their story-pictures. 'One picture stimulus was perceived most often as a man in an airplane reclining seat returning from a business trip or conference. A high IQ student gave the following story: "Mr. Smith is on his way home from a successful business trip. He is very happy and he is thinking about his wonderful family and how glad he will be to see them again. He can picture it, about an hour from now, his plane landing at the airport and

Mrs. Smith and their three children all there welcoming him home again." A high-creative subject wrote this story: "This man is flying back from Reno, where he has just won a divorce from his wife. He couldn't stand to live with her any more, he told the judge, because she wore so much cold cream on her face at night that her head would skid across the pillow and hit him in the head. He is now contemplating a new skid-proof face cream.'"

"This is perhaps sufficient to illustrate the contrasting cognitive styles of Getzels' and Jackson's high creatives and high IQ's, and also to suggest what it is that teachers dislike about the former. The youngsters in their high-creative sample *do* disrupt the social environment. You can lead them to the pot; but they just don't melt, they burn. Intelligent and perceptive critics of Getzels' and Jackson's work have pointed out that the actual power of the creative students to create anything worthwhile remains, at their age, unestablished; but their prickliness, hostility, and aggression show up on nearly every instrument of the study. Getzels and Jackson included among their procedures one of having each subject draw whatever he liked on a sheet of paper captioned 'Playing Tag in the School Yard.' The drawings of the high-IQ subjects are literal and humorless, 'stimulus-bound'; the high-creatives' drawings are fantastic and comical, with something of the quality of Till Eulenspiegel about them, but they are also gory. Combining Getzels' and Jackson's Tables 10 and 11, we get the following statistics on these drawings as they rate them:

	TYPE OF STUDENT	
	High *IQ*	*High* *Creative*
Number of students in sample	28	26
Humor present	5	14
Humor absent	23	12
Violence present	1	9
Violence absent	27	17

"We do not, of course, know how this spiral of reciprocal hostility starts; whether the youngsters become hostile and sarcastic because they are punished for their originality, even though at first they express it openly, innocently, and warmly, or whether a youngster will only think and feel divergently if he starts with a certain detachment from and distrust of conventional, established attitudes and procedures. Most likely — say, on the basis of such a cogent analysis as that in Ernest G. Schachtel's brilliant and classic paper, 'On Memory and Childhood Amnesia,'[5] the beginnings of creativity in the exploratory sensuality of childhood are quite free from hostility; they are innocent, though hardly chaste. But exploratory sensuality is punished long before the child gets to school, and certainly before he gets to high school. Among the initially gifted, the high creatives are perhaps those who have received enough affection through the total process that they can afford to respond to insult by getting angry and verbally swatting back. The high IQ's have been treated almost wholly as instruments

5. Included in *Metamorphosis* (New York: Basic Books, Inc., 1959), pp. 279-322.

of parental aspirations, even at home, and become anxious at any sign they are getting off the track; anger, and hostility are beyond their emotional means. The findings of Getzels and Jackson on the home background of their contrasting subjects bear this out.

"But their most poignant data were obtained from an instrument they called the Outstanding Traits Test. This consisted of 13 thumbnail descriptions of such traits as social skill, goal-directedness, and good marks, using phrases like 'Here is the student who is best able to look at things in a new way and to discover new ideas'; 'Here is the student who is best at getting along with other people'; 'Here is the outstanding athlete in the school,' and so forth. The students in their sample were asked to rank those 13 descriptions in three different ways: as 'preferred for oneself,' as 'favored by teachers,' and as 'believed predictive of adult success.' The rank-order correlations obtained between the high-IQ and high-creative students as to how these traits contributed to later success was *unity;* as to what teachers preferred, it was 0.98. The high-creative and high-IQ students, in short, were in absolute agreement as to what traits would make a person succeed in adult life; they were virtually agreed as to what teachers liked in students – though the two ratings were not identical. Nevertheless, the correlation between the two groups' ratings of these traits as 'preferred for oneself' was only 0.41. This can only be interpreted to mean that one or both of these groups believed that pleasing teachers and becoming successful was just not worth what it cost, even though they agreed completely as to what that cost would be.

"Which group rejected the image of success that both shared? The data clearly permit me to resolve this question and end your suspense. Here, instead of correlations *between* the high IQ's and the high creatives, we need, of course, correlations *within* each group for the three possible bases of sorting. Here they are:

	High IQ	High Creative
Components of Correlation		
Personal traits believed 'predictive of success' and 'favored by teachers'	0.62	0.59
Personal traits 'preferred for oneself' and 'believed predictive of adult success'	0.81	0.10
Personal traits 'preferred for oneself' and 'believed favored by teachers'	0.67	−0.25

"I would interpret these statistics to mean that the high creatives cannot bring themselves to be what they believe success requires, and are even more strongly repelled by what the teacher demands. The correlation coefficients on the two 'favored by teachers' categories are really very curious and interesting across the board. I find a 0.6 correlation here astonishingly low for *both* groups — with these N's of 26 and 28 such a correlation has little statistical significance. While, for the high IQ's, the correlation between 'preferred for oneself' was only 0.41. This can only be infor the high creatives, it is negligible.

"All these data could be explained very satisfactorily by the hypothesis that the high creatives, spontaneous and joyful as the happy-go-lucky Negro slave of song and story, just don't give a damn; that this is their way of singing 'Hallelujah, I'm a bum.' But it won't do. Using two standard measures of the need to achieve, David McClelland's *need: achievement* and Fred L. Strodtbeck's *V-score*, Getzels and Jackson were unable to find any significant differences between the two groups, or between either group and the total population of 449; the figures given for the high creatives are actually slightly higher on both measures. So we must turn for our interpretation to the relationship between the students and the school itself.

"Both groups, I infer, see the teacher as on the side of success but being too naive and square to be a very reliable guide as to how to go after it. Since the high IQ's are determined to *be* the kind of person who succeeds, this reduces the relevance of the teacher to him, but not the relevance of the school. Or to put it another way, the importance of the school as the monitor of his progress is quite enough to bring the high IQ to terms with it; and the terms are generous enough not to demand that he listen to what it actually says. To the high creative, the whole experience is rather frustrating and annoying, and relevant only because there is no viable alternative to high school for a middle-class adolescent. . . ."

My own recent research strongly complements that of Getzels and Jackson in showing teachers to be just as much opposed to divergent thinking or highly creative youngsters as the students in Getzels' and Jackson's sample thought they were. The relevant parts of this study, which I did in collaboration with two colleagues at Brooklyn College, Carl Nordstrom and Hilary Gold,[6] included 246 students and 55 teachers at seven public and two private secondary schools spread along the east coast from Florida to upstate New York. Both the students and the teachers, in a procedure in which they were interviewed in some depth, strongly disparaged youngsters of high competence and autonomy but idiosyncratic personal style, favoring with depressing consistency what they called well-rounded individuals who were popular on campus and displayed superficial social skills. In this particular procedure they were asked to select from brief descriptions of nine fictitious high school students those who would be best — or worst — to include in a delegation to be sent to the state capital at the request of a visiting monarch, who had expressed a desire to meet some "spirited young people." Our subjects were directed to select students who would represent what was "best and finest about the school" but were left free to make this judgment on any basis they chose.

Both students and teachers in our sample give creativity a hard time. They rejected candidates who were good at *particular* things. *No* student, and only two teachers, thought this girl would be best to send.

NANCY HARRIS

Nancy Harris is a violinist. This year, she has been accorded the signal honor of being first violinist and concert master of the all-state orchestra. She

6. *Society's Children: A Study of Ressentiment in the Secondary School* (New York: Random House, 1967).

has also performed as soloist for several of the local symphony orchestras. Nancy is gifted with artistic sensibility and quickness in all things. She is a very good student and still manages to keep her coursework up while practicing three or four hours a day. Unfortunately, her schedule does not allow much opportunity for social activity, which is too bad because she really is an attractive young lady who, with a little effort, could easily be more popular. But her enthusiasms are more for things than for people, and she prefers artistic creation to success with her fellow students.

But 109 of our student subjects and 20 of our teachers thought that Karen Clarke would be the best person to send, making her the favorite of both groups by a wide margin:

Karen Clarke

Karen Clarke will be giving the valedictory at graduation for this year's class. As she should. Always well-groomed and polite, she is completely in command of herself in any situation. She is the perfect model of what a high school student ought to be. Her work is neat, correct, and, unlike that of so many other students', in on time. It really has to be because her dad, Mr. Clarke, teaches here and he makes sure Karen doesn't get any special favors. He makes certain that she stands up for herself and does her work. In student activities she is Treasurer of the Senior Class. She is also a teacher's aide for Mr. Pottitone's chemistry laboratory and a member of the Ethics Committee of the Student Government. Where others are concerned, Karen always tries to be helpful. She wants to go to a good college like Vassar or Smith and plans everything she does carefully, with this in mind. At Le Moyne everybody feels that she has a real chance to get into the kind of college she would like to go to.

In contrast, two of the most frequently rejected of the nine fictitious students were boys we described as possessing several highly developed skills that they practice, however, rather erratically as the spirit moves them. One of these is drawn as a star debater and first-string basketball starter; the other as a near-genius in mathematics, editor of the school literary magazine, and chess champion who "does manage to argue with some of his teachers. If it wasn't for this, he would probably be valedictorian of his class. He has the ability to be." In both cases the autonomy of these boys was specifically held against them by many of our respondents, whether student or teacher. They were seen as underachievers who lacked self-discipline; they only did what they felt like doing and therefore, in contrast to Karen, were not to be trusted.

Thus far, I have referred only to the ways in which the responses of students and of teachers to the episode we called "The King's Visit" in our research protocol were similar. The fact that they were so similar is itself, I believe, as important as the quality of the response, for the similarity establishes that the school, in its attitude toward creative self-expression, has an animus of its own that both transcends and utilizes the characteristics of its teachers. Nevertheless, there were significant differences. The teachers who took part in our study — not a random sample, as our students were, but individuals identified by colleagues as especially influential in the school — were less strongly anti-intellectual than our student subjects, on the average. They more often indicated that they valued academic achievement, though they preferred to see it expressed in neat, polite ways, and placed less value on social skills. To counterbalance this slight tendency to support at least conventional excellence, our teachers were also more aggressively committed to an egalitarian ideology; even more than the students, they seemed to resent special creative gifts as unfair advantages to be disparaged as un-American in principle. Where our student subjects would more frequently have avoided unusual talent and sensitivity as something that might make you unpopular and get you into trouble — as, indeed, it may — the teachers who took part in our study rather more often actively resented the possibility of exceptional talent and were determined to resist in advance any special claims it might make on its own behalf. But this difference is only one of emphasis, not a real contrast. The attitudes expressed by teachers and students overlapped far more than they differed; and each in their own way showed a permanent, sullen, antagonism toward the creative.

Any attempt to improve instruction in the humanities so as to contribute more to the development of creativity in youngsters, then, runs counter to the preferences and values of a predominance of the typical school staff. There are, however, certain countervailing tendencies in the schools. For one thing, there are many good and sensitive teachers who like free and expressive behavior in students and will support it as far as they can within the system; improved curricula and techniques do permit them to support it further before they get into conflict with their colleagues or the administration. Furthermore, secondary school teachers, like college instructors, are supported by the norms of their discipline, though much more feebly. Exceptional contributions to education in the humanities enhance their professional reputation; they, too, get to attend national meetings of their kind if they publish and thereby gain the usual rewards.

But such factors as these are not enough to offset the fact that inadequate instruction in the humanities is not a consequence of ineptitude or failure but is positively functional for public education in our society, which binds us together by concealing the insights which divide and placating members of social groups with real conflicts of interest. Potentially excellent humanities teachers themselves constitute such a group, in the context of the school system, whose interests, insofar as they favor the development of sharp and courageous youngsters, conflict with the purpose and function of the school. In a pluralistic society, democratic in form, like ours, such conflicts are usually resolved by concession rather than suppression so far as they can be. And what happens in this case is usually that the curricular innovation is adopted but is institutionalized in such a way as to limit its influence on thought and behavior outside the classroom or the studio. This, I should judge, is the most important reason why curricular improvements tend to remain gimmicky and fuse slowly, if at all, into the customary structure of American education; grafts implanted on an alien species usually die or remain sterile.

It is difficult, therefore, for me to accede with any self-confidence to Dr. Taylor's suggestion that we "write about what we would like to see happen in the experience of young people which, in our judgment, would raise the level of their sensitivity to every kind of value question, both inside and outside the school system, to give them a chance for direct confrontation with works of art of their own making and of others." There isn't much difficulty in defining what I would like to see happen. I would like to see schools run with respect for the privacy and dignity of their students, on schedules flexible enough to permit people to finish what they have started without being constantly inter-rupted. I would like to see schools in which teachers of the arts as a matter of firm policy began their work with students by probing for the meanings the student was seeking to express, but then continued to partici-pate in the ensuing creative process by a very firm insistence on the student facing and doing his best to solve the technical problems which cannot be evaded by enthusiasm. But this implies that some of the stu-dents who crave success with an addict's craving and a starving man's need would nevertheless experience failure; and that some of the literature and objects created would be proudly accepted and exhibited even if obscene. In schools with more liberal social climates, it would also mean that some works would be *rejected*, even though they were obscene and showed a commendable devotion to the cause of civil rights.

What I want to see happen is for youngsters to experience the private vision that any one, to the degree that he is an artist, must start with: the discipline, derived from the properties of his medium and from the nature of the available symbols, to which the artist must submit; and the growth and development of that vision under discipline. But a public school, socializing young Americans to enjoy the Great Society, is not a very promising ambience in which to try to bring this confrontation about.

Some Ideas for Action

HAROLD TAYLOR

As THE READER WILL HAVE OBSERVED, along with the general observations, criticism, and analysis by the members of the Symposium, quite a few practical suggestions were made by those present at the Symposium about what to do with the arts and humanities in the schools. In what follows, I have summarized the main suggestions and recommendations and have added some of my own, in the hope that these might be useful to teachers and others who are at work in the arts in education.

1. The most general suggestion, and one which kept coming up in the discussion, was that educators needed to break down the distinction between art as an academic subject and art as it is practiced by artists. Whenever art is taught, unless it is to be mistaught, the teacher should be an artist. That is to say, he should be

a person whose education and experience has involved him in creative work and performance in the field in which he is teaching, whether or not he has actually been a professional in creative work or in performance.

The professionals should be related to the universities, schools, and colleges in every way possible, as performers and teachers, so that students can be brought directly in touch with the living arts as they are practiced by genuine artists.

2. This means, among other things, at least two main courses of action for educators: first, the reform of teacher education programs to give enough time and curriculum in the student's schedule to allow for the full development of his interests and talents in the arts; and secondly, the appointment of practicing artists in all fields to the faculties of the colleges of education. Either do this or authorize joint appointments to the colleges of education and the art, music, theatre, dance, painting, sculpture, and design departments, so that promising young performers and artists can learn to teach the arts while they are learning to work with them.

For example, there is no reason why a college or high school student who plays the clarinet beautifully, or is a good dancer, actor, or composer, should not teach his art in the local schools, to elementary or high school students, either during regular class periods or after school is out, forming jazz groups, theatre groups, poetry clubs, or painting centers, as a regular part of his college curriculum in education and art. He will discover more about his own art as he takes on the task of teaching it to others, and the fact that he too is a student makes it easier to organize both informal and formal groups of students because of the easy and direct relations he can establish with those not very much younger than himself.

On the other hand, there is no reason why professional artists in the local community could not teach the arts in the local schools. For example, a choral conductor or chamber director whose main preoccupation is in giving concerts could form groups of singers and players in the schools, sometimes in collaboration with the musicians in the community. Robert Shaw spoke of this in his paper and in the Symposium discussion; in his own work, Shaw has mixed together professional singers and musicians with college and high school students very successfully. The same approach can be taken to painting, sculpture, and graphic design, with collaboration among the artists, the museum directors, and the school teachers.

3. An extension of this idea is possible through sending groups of talented students, from college and from high school, around the state to put on plays, give concerts, exhibit their paintings and talk about them, with an exchange program of visiting faculty artists as well as exchange of students. Just as it is common practice to put local football teams into a bus or two once a week during the season and take them off for performances in other communities, it should become common practice to have the students perform for each other at student theatre, dance, and music festivals on a regular basis during the academic year. Naturally the schedule would have to be loosened up to allow this to take place, but since it seems comparatively easy to rearrange

schedules for athletic performances, it should be fairly simple to do it for regular subjects in the school and college arts curriculum.

4.   Robert Shaw has suggested forming a whole series of chamber groups—woodwind quintets, string trios, quartets, brass ensembles, small choruses, madrigal groups, mixed choruses—with a fully developed repertory of musical works chosen for their intrinsic merit. To this I would like to add the suggestion that a regular part of the curriculum should include composition by students for their friends the musicians—short pieces for trios and chamber groups of all kinds, jazz pieces, and choral works, all of them related to dance groups and theatre music. From our experience at Sarah Lawrence College I draw the suggestion that students in poetry, theatre, literature, and dance should combine forces, for example, by students writing poems to be danced, other students setting the poems to music for the dancers, composing choral works to be danced, writing music for short theatre experiments, electronically-inclined students writing music for mixed-media happenings, and others using tape recorders to make sound tracks for slide projections and 8 millimeter films.

5.   Or, starting from the theatre side, students could be invited to do short one-act or one-scene plays for which painters and sculptors could be asked to design stage sets and decor and composers and electronic-tape-recorder experimenters could be asked to write the music for snatches of dialogue written in literature class.

6.   In connection with the development of school pro-

grams in the creative arts, classes in literature could be asked to write reviews of the works which other students had created and/or performed, with class discussions of the works themselves and the reviews which had been written about them, preferably with the original artist and performers present. Acting improvisations could become a regular part of literature classes.

7. Among Stephen Spender's suggestions were that each student should write an essay on a general subject once a week, "some might take the form of communications from one discipline to another." The history teacher or the science teacher, for example, would read the best student essays, and both classes could meet to discuss them. One day a term or a year should be set aside when a teacher from one of the disciplines would explain to a school audience of students and teachers what he thought was the meaning and importance of his work.

8. Harold Rosenberg suggests starting with the university as a "training ground for artists as well as for art teachers. Those who are going to make art and those who are going to educate people about it should be studying side by side." Art history should be studied in relation to religion, philosophy, mathematics, politics, biology, fashion, social history, and psychology, and in relation to the student's actual work in the art itself.

9. Stanley Kauffmann suggests that since the film is available to the classroom exactly as it came from the filmmaker's hand, the presentation of some of the film masterpieces (not educational films *about* art) should

be a major teaching instrument in the arts. The early exposure to good films in the schools creates an audience which can demand high standards in the future, not only for films but for all the other arts.

Although we did not discuss the idea at length during the Symposium, it was clear that we were all very much in favor of a serious expansion of the art of student filmmaking, to allow writers, artists, composers with sound-tapes, actors, stage designers, and everyone else a chance to experiment in new kinds of expression. To this might be added the use of photography and of video-tape for recording improvised acting, discussions, visiting teachers from other classes, or any other event which could be turned into a starting point for discussion of the arts and philosophy.

10. There is room for radical expansion of the idea of bringing the arts from the schools and colleges into the streets and into the community, with the school considered a community center for the nurture and development of the arts. This would argue for street-corner theatre, organized by students in the community, church-basement poetry centers, store-front sculpture studios, and the development of a natural literature of stories, poetry, plays, and writing from the community itself, all of which could be used as a central component in the art program and the curriculum of the school.

11. Last, but not finally, I recommend the full use of books, articles, stories, experiences, television programs (to be reviewed as to content, style, and significance) local museums, theatres, concerts, and all other occa-

sions and materials which lie outside the school itself, with a serious effort made by teachers to make use of the full range of contemporary culture outside the school to invigorate the regular studies of the school and college classroom.

If, in the beginning of such new efforts it is necessary to find the time for the arts and the humanities outside the regular classroom schedule, then start things there, secure in the faith that the enthusiasm and aesthetic energy of the students will carry the ideas from there straight into the curriculum itself. There is enough potential energy available for creative purposes in all of us to make certain that once the aesthetic impulse is released, it will carry the arts not only into the school curriculum, but to the ends of the earth.

Contributors

Edgar Friedenberg

Prior to his present position as Professor of Sociology and Social Education at the State University of New York at Buffalo, Dr. Friedenberg taught at the University of California (Davis), the University of Chicago, and Brooklyn College. He received his degrees from Centenary College, B.S., Stanford University, M.A., and the University of Chicago, Ph.D.

His articles appear in a number of periodicals, including the *New York Review of Books, Commentary, New Republic, The New York Times Sunday Magazine*, and scholarly journals. His books include *The Vanishing Adolescent, Coming of Age in America, The Dignity of Youth and Other Atavisms*, and *Society's Children: A Study of Ressentiment in the Secondary School*. Dr. Friedenberg serves on various national committees and studies, lectures frequently at colleges and universities, and has completed two research projects for the U.S. Office of Education.

STANLEY KAUFFMANN

A graduate of New York University's College of Fine Arts, Mr. Kauffmann spent a number of years in a repertory company concerned primarily with Shakespeare. He has published a number of one-act plays and has written seven novels, including *The Hidden Hero, A Change of Climate,* and *Man of the World.*

In recent years he has been particularly active as a critic. From 1958 until 1966 he was film critic of the *New Republic;* then, after eight months as drama critic of *The New York Times,* he returned to the *New Republic* as leading book reviewer and cultural commentator. In December 1967 he resumed his post as film critic of that magazine.

For four years Mr. Kauffmann conducted a weekly television program, *The Art of Film,* on New York's education station. He has been made an honorary fellow of Morse College of Yale University for his film criticism in general. His collection, *A World on Film,* was published by Harper & Row in 1966 and has since appeared in a Delta Books paperback edition. He was the first chairman of the National Society of Film Critics.

Mr. Kauffmann's literary criticism has appeared in numerous journals, and he is the author of the essay on literature in *The Great Idea Today 1964.* He has lectured at numerous colleges and universities and in 1967-68 was Visiting Professor of Drama at Yale University.

HAROLD ROSENBERG

Mr. Rosenberg has been active as an art and literary critic and as an author since the 1930's. His works have appeared in *The New Yorker, Art News, Vogue, Commentary, Partisan Review, Les Temps Modernes,* and numerous other periodicals in the United States and abroad. He is art critic of *The New Yorker.*

His books include *Trance Above the Streets* (poems), *The Anxious Object, Arshile Gorky,* and *Tradition of the New.* Among his other works is an introduction to Marcel Raymond's *From Baudelaire to Surrealism.*

Mr. Rosenberg has conducted the Christian Gauss Seminar at Princeton University, the Baldwin Seminar at Oberlin, and has been Regents Lecturer at the University of California, Berkeley. In 1964, he received the Frank Jewett Mather Award of the College Art Association. He was Visiting Professor and Artist-in-Residence at Southern Illinois University in 1965 and is now Professor of the Committee on Social Thought at the University of Chicago.

ROBERT SHAW

Starting as conductor of his college glee club, Mr. Shaw went on to found the Fred Waring Glee Club and in 1948 organized the Robert Shaw Chorale. With this new ensemble, he toured the Middle East, Scandinavia, and Europe under the auspices of the U.S. Department of State in 1956. Another tour for the State Department took place between October and January 1961-62, when he made his first tour of the Soviet Union. Following was a third tour for the State Department in 1964; this time Mr. Shaw took his Chorale to South America.

Mr. Shaw has served as Director of Choral Music at the Juilliard School of Music and the Berkshire Music Center; since 1956 he has been codirector of the Alaska Festival of Music; from 1953 to 1957 Mr. Shaw was conductor of the San Diego Symphony. During the summers of 1965-67, he was instrumental in establishing the Meadow Brook School of Music, near Detroit, in conjunction with the Meadow Brook Festival, where he lectured, conducted, and served as its Director of the Choral and Orchestral Institutes. He has appeared as guest conductor with the Minneapolis Symphony, Detroit Symphony, Boston Symphony Orchestra, New York Philharmonic Orchestra, Chicago Symphony Orchestra, National Symphony, and others.

In 1956, at the invitation of George Szell, Mr. Shaw became Associate Conductor of the Cleveland Orchestra. In addition to organizing and preparing the Cleveland Orchestra Chorus, he was responsible for a number of subscription concerts, educational concerts, and tour concerts. Mr. Shaw assumed his new position as Music Director and Conductor of the Atlanta Symphony Orchestra in August 1967.

STEPHEN SPENDER

Mr. Spender began writing poetry early in life; his first book of poems, *Nine Experiments*, was printed on his own handpress in London in 1928, when he was eighteen. Another volume, *Twenty Poems*, appeared while he was still an undergraduate at Oxford. Other volumes include *Ruins and Visions, Poems of Dedication, The Edge of Being*, and *Selected Poems* (1964). He is also a novelist, short-story writer, critic, dramatist, editor, lecturer, and translator of a number of literary works. Writings include *The Backward Son, The Creative Element*, and *Trial of a Judge*. Until 1967 he was coeditor of *Encounter*.

Mr. Spender has served as Counselor, Section of Letters, UNESCO; Chair of Poetry at the University of Cincinnati; Beckman Professor in the Department of English at the University of California, Berkeley; and Visiting Professor of English at Northwestern University.

During the 1965-66 term, he was Consultant in Poetry in English to the Library of Congress and has recently completed the 1968 Mellon Lectures on Imagination in Poetry and Painting.

HAROLD TAYLOR

Before accepting the presidency of Sarah Lawrence College in 1945, a post he held for fourteen years, Harold Taylor was a member of the faculty in philosophy at the University of Wisconsin where he taught courses in the philosophy of the arts, social theory, and the philosophy of James, Santayana, and Dewey. His doctorate degree was awarded by the University of London for work in the relation of philosophy to literature. Under his administration at Sarah Lawrence College, new curricula were developed in graduate studies, teacher education, and the performing arts, and a new Arts Center, designed by Marcel Breuer, was constructed on the campus.

Dr. Taylor has served as President of the American Ballet Theatre Foundation and is presently a member of the Board of Directors of the National Repertory Theatre, the Martha Graham School of Contemporary Dance, the Putney School, and is a member of the Executive Committee of the National Committee for Support of the Public Schools. He is the author of *Art and the Intellect, On Education and Freedom,* editor and coauthor of *Essays in Teaching,* and editor of *The Idea of a World University.* His work appears in philosophical and educational journals and anthologies as well as in *The New York Times Sunday Magazine,* the *Saturday Review, Look,* and other magazines. Dr. Taylor has recently completed a two-year study of the education of teachers in world affairs, to be published in the fall of 1968; he is presently lecturing in colleges and universities and writing a book on the arts and education.